Poor Bloody Bunny

JERRY MCNUTT

DEDICATION

This book is dedicated to all my friends and family, especially Mom.

CONTENTS

INTRODUCTION

Odds are you've never heard of me but there's a good chance you're somewhat familiar with my work. I've been writing, producing, and directing television for ten years. Naturally, you're wondering what shows I produced that you might have stumbled across while channel surfing. Remember that time you stayed out drinking and the next day you woke up with a thunderous hangover? You walked into the living room, lowered the blinds because the sun was too bright, and sprawled out on the couch to try to get some rest. Just as you closed your eyes, that asshole neighbor started mowing the lawn at 11:00 in the morning. You then needed some white noise to drown out the mower but didn't want to watch anything too stimulating because you really needed more sleep. Click, click, click...there it is...HGTV. The network dedicated to helping home owners maintain their private little piece of earth with a steady stream of sedating infotainment. It's a great channel to learn about the basics of home improvement...or to let your stressed out mind relax, take a break from the bombardment of violence and aggression found on other channels and simply take a serene nap on your couch – if only that asshole neighbor would mow his damn lawn at a respectable freaking hour of the blessed day!

I've written many screenplays and produced a handful of short films. As soon as I finish one project, I begin writing another. Why? I love writing. I'm passionate about people. Why we act the way we do, how we justify bizarre behavior, who we think we are or who we believe we have the potential to eventually become. We are, all of us, fascinating, infuriating, intriguing, insufferable, and ultimately, in some strange way, in some hidden place, wonderful beyond words. When we blow a fuse, when we fall in love, when we stand up to fight or lay down in defeat, we are truly captivating. The decisions we make and why we make them are why the world spins at such a great speed, slightly tilted on its axis.

The Bible says something like "above all things there is hope." Hope, in its nurturing or in its demise, is the foundation of all our decisions. Hope affects each of us differently. It transforms some into fanatics and drives others with passionate endurance. What ever hope is, it's the one thing that allows us to do ridiculously amazing things. For instance, did you know that someone went to the moon? I'm not kidding. Sure, you've heard that Neil Armstrong went to the moon but did you ever really stop to think about the level of hope that it took to even begin planning such an undertaking? How much hope would you need to tie yourself to a rocket that launches you up only 100 feet? Half mile? What about riding that same rocket into the stratosphere? To zoom into space hoping that the thousands of things that could go wrong wouldn't? To step outside the protective shell of your spacecraft and place your foot where no human had ever been before? To begin the journey back? To survive re-entry and the crash into an ocean? Folks, that's a giant boat-load of collective hope.

I remember seeing a photograph of a Chinese man standing defiantly in front of a convoy of tanks. One ordinary, yet uncommonly brave soul was able to bring an entire army to a halt. To the best of my knowledge, that individual remains anonymous but his example of hope will live forever. Conversely, I once watched a little boy, six or seven years old, cursing at his grandmother in a mall. The little shit was ripping her a new one with words that I didn't incorporate until my early thirties. When his words caused no reaction, he began hitting her. I instantly pictured this child's drunken, mullet wearing, tattooed, cigarette smoking, gun-totting dad behaving the same way. The grandmother never flinched. Why? Hope. She had hope that if she didn't react with aggression that her grandson might learn that he wouldn't have to either. Granted, the boy could have used at least one good smack to the head, but I have hope that the old lady persevered and made a difference in little Johnny's life. If not, tell the neighbors to hide their cats cause that little nutter is going to be a new kind of crazy.

The backdrop of the stories you are about to read is predominately my hometown of Ozark, Arkansas, but, with the exception of a couple of embarrassingly countrified tales, could be anywhere. The stories reveal a great deal about me but even more about you. By you, I mean us... who we are...all of us. You will laugh. You might cry. You'll probably shake your head in disgust and most likely have your gag reflex triggered at least twice. You'll most certainly nod with familiarity. My hope is that you will be highly entertained and profoundly moved. If hope is the greatest of things, then what better nourishment could hope have than laughter? Most of the stories in this collection could easily be sad or pathetic. However, God blessed me with a bizarre view of the world and the ability to see things from the perspective of others. Admittedly, my perspective of others is sometimes completely self-serving to simply enhance my own view of our tiny planet, but it makes my sky bluer and keeps me from burning buildings and stealing fruit.

The characters that you are about to meet are some of the most amazing, profound, inspiring, borderline retarded, overly aggressive, humble, confused, misguided, socially backward, religiously manipulative, physically blessed, and emotionally mundane people on Earth. I present these stories to illustrate two basic truths. The first truth is that regardless of your background or experiences, you are the one that chooses the path you will travel. The second truth is that if you are willing to see things a little sideways, you can laugh at anything, no matter how absurd, unfair, mean, or down right shitty that life throws at you.

I've had many trusted friends, as well as a handful of strangers read various drafts as I wrote for hours upon hours digging through my memory for the best nuggets in the deepest, most repressed corners of my mind. Of all the reviews that came back, one stands out above all others. My mother passed the collection to a friend of hers who returned the next morning, having read the entire book, and admitted that she laughed so hard that she accidentally peed on herself. I was humbled beyond belief and encouraged that my work might truly make someone's day a little lighter.

As you read the following words, embrace hope, believe in yourself, ignore doubters, make your voice heard, get mad enough to make a change, and, by all means, laugh so hard that you pee in your pants.

ZOMBIE HANDS

When was the last time you heard a good haunted house story? Every town or village across the globe claims to have an old home with a super natural connection. There's always something gruesome and freaky about the previous owner or a stranger passing through who was denied bread and water. Haunted houses are complete b.s. and everyone knows it. Yet, we all love a good haunted house story, especially when the person telling the story swears it's true and was even a witness to the spooky events. Still, how do people buy into ridiculous events that have not a shred of scientific evidence? Hogwash, I say!

But my haunted house story is completely true, and I was witness to each disturbing event. No kidding. The following events unfolded before my very eyes. The story I'm about to share took place over the course of a few months. In the end, I lived. As I type these words, I am alive. But there was a death. It was a tragic and senseless death. The demise was slow and painful. To this day, no decision has been made as to whether the catastrophe was a suicide or a homicide. We may never know…but the story endures and the haunting continues. Read on…if you dare!

It was the fall of 1986 and the Hillbilly football season was in high gear. School had only started up a few weeks earlier so the newness of classes, teachers, etc., was still enough to get excited about. Some guys were taller, some girls were fuller, things were changing and change was always good. Living in such a small, isolated town, we rarely had new students. But this year we had one, Psycho Shawn. Psycho didn't arrive at student orientation with the cool nickname. He earned it. Being a new kid in school, one only has a couple of choices: let some time pass and sooner or later you'll fit in, or prove to everyone that you're crazy, and people will want to hang around with you because you're so stinkin' intense. Psycho, as the moniker implies, chose door number two.

Psycho hit the ground running. In addition to being incredibly smart (Psycho developed his own calculus formula which the teacher refused to let him use because it only worked 90% of the time – which meant he could only earn an "A"), he was also a very talented long distance runner. Endurance training was a part of football practice and Psycho quickly earned a reputation as a great runner. So much so that the football players would often report to me, the reigning district champion of the half-mile, that I was going to be getting my ass kicked when track season rolled around in the spring. When I finally met the running legend, he was introduced as, "…the guy I've been telling you about." Psycho had also been told about me and seemed to look forward to the challenge of competing against each other. Personally, I was very happy with my track times and wanted no reason to work any harder than I already was. Track sucked and I only ran because I was expected to do it as another means of supporting my high school. Let me say again, track sucks. Lots of pain, cramps, sweating, fainting, fatigue… it sucks. But there was also a female track team and I enjoyed hanging out with girls in shorts.

The moment Psycho earned his nickname is clear to all of those who were in my 2:00 pm Spanish class. Shawn (I'll continue to refer to him as Psycho in just a few moments) was hunched over the top of his desk with his arms underneath the desk gripping the front edge from below. His forehead was touching the desk and he was flexing his entire body with so much force that he appeared to be having a seizure. He was also holding his breath, and had been for about a minute. My friends and I knew he was getting ready to do something to show off but had no idea what in the hell was going on. Finally, the nervousness of everyone watching made its way to Ms. Instructera. Her first instinct was right on target with ours, this guy was doing something stupid for attention. "Shawn," she said with slight frustration. He didn't move. Her second instinct was also right on target with ours…that something really weird was about to happen.

"Shawn…?" There was a notable unease to her second attempt as she made a cautious move forward. Goofing around in class was always a fine idea, but ignoring the teacher was virtually unheard of. As she took her next step forward, all of the students made a slight adjustment away from Shawn. "Shawn, I'm talking to you." Nothing. Twenty sets of eyes, forty eyes total, began darting back and forth in anticipation. Finally, Ms. Instructera had decided *no mas*. She put her bravest foot forward, determined to regain the attention of her students. Just as she reached out to touch Shawn's shoulder, he slowly lifted his head. By now, Shawn had been holding his breath for close to two minutes. His eyes were bloodshot and every vein in his purple head was swollen and throbbing like a pit full of vipers with bellies full of live rats. He glared at the unsuspecting teacher through the top of his eye sockets, his head down but tilted freakishly to the side. As if the moment weren't sinister enough, Shawn's tongue was stretched out of his mouth and arching toward his nose as he released a ghastly and demonic hissing sound. Shocked beyond all sense of reason and holy rationale, Ms. Instructera staggered back with her hands over mouth, turned and fled the classroom.

To be honest, I don't remember my own reaction or that of my fellow students. If the above incident were a movie, the editor would cut to a scene at recess where the students are saying things like, "Damn, that was weird!" Or, possibly, the movie classroom would erupt in cheers. But Ms. Instructera was actually a pretty cool teacher, and, from what I remember, was also kinda hot. I have a feeling that we all simply sat in silence while Shawn giggled at his own audacity. Eventually, I suppose the bell rang and we all left for the next class whispering something like, "Damn, that was weird!" Regardless, that was the birth of Psycho Shawn.

A few weeks later, Wayne and I discovered a creepy, old house in the woods while hiking. (Wow, I guess these stories really do start off that way! Again I say, true story.) Days later, we were telling our friend John just how creepy the place was. He started calling us a couple of chicken shits and claimed he would spend the night in the house all by himself. We all laughed at his bravado knowing he was completely full of poo. Regardless, Wayne and I decided to show John, and a few other buddies, the house later that night.

Wayne, John, Alan, Psycho, and I ventured into the dark woods just beyond the city limits around 10:00 o'clock. After hiking for about twenty minutes, we came to a clearing. We stood shoulder to shoulder looking at a very imposing silhouette. Of course, it was a full moon, but the scary thing was that the house looked exactly like the house on Amityville horror (two-story, lots of windows, pointy roof) and the barn behind the house was just like the barn that Jason died in at the end of Friday the 13th part 4 or 5. (Keep in mind that I'm not making this up!) At the sight of the house, John immediately confessed, "There's no way in hell I'm spending the night in that thing." After laughing at John's cowardice, we all stood motionless for a few minutes lamenting that none of us had been smart enough to bring a flashlight. Finally, we ventured forward, all talking about how cool it would be to go inside if we only had a light of some sort. Damn the luck! We'd just have to wait another day to explore the scary-ass, abandoned, lunatic-sheltering, ghost-riddled mansion.

Soon enough, the inevitable happened. Wayne dared John to go inside by himself for fifteen minutes. We all laughed and then John dared Alan. Alan called John a pussy just as Psycho interrupted us all with, "I'll go." Without any further prompting, Psycho walked into the dark house completely alone.

None of us could really believe that Psycho went in by his lonesome. While we waited in the security of the group, we joked that he was probably just standing by the front door, too scared to venture further. Besides, it was a full moon which meant there was just enough light that it really wasn't all that scary anyway. Still, I think we were all wondering why Psycho went in. Was it just to outdo us all, to prove he was the bravest or to enhance his crazy reputation? We didn't discourage him, so, maybe our stunned silence at his offer was interpreted as encouragement.

Fifteen minutes went by and we joked that he would be bounding out any moment. A few minutes later and we started to worry. I whispered his name, "Psycho?"

Alan whispered, "Why are we whispering?" I whispered back, "Shut up!"

Wayne pointed to the staircase, and we all saw Psycho slowly ascending to the second floor. This was serious. We were already silently freaking out that Psycho had dared to enter the house, but now that he was walking as if being summoned…that's just too much for a group of teenagers who know full well what happens to teenagers who go into the woods to goof on a supposed haunted house. After what seemed like an eerily long time, Psycho returned. We gathered around and asked, "What was it like?" What did you see?" Without interrupting his stride, he walked past the group. "I don't want to talk about it." He continued walking right into the woods. We rushed to follow, but hardly a word was spoken the entire way back.

Of course, the story of Psycho Shawn and the haunted house spread quickly, and a few more of our friends wanted to romp through the woods as soon as the sun set. Even girls wanted to go, which meant that the entire tone of the upcoming evening had completely changed. Psycho and I decided to go out to the property early, find a great hiding spot, and scare the pants off the girls. Psycho and I arrived just before the sun set. We went upstairs and sat in a ratty bedroom that offered a great view of the wooded area from which the unsuspecting group would soon tiptoe toward us.

It's important to understand the layout of the upstairs to be thoroughly terrified by what's about to happen. I'll make this brief so try to stay with me – draw if you must. Imagine one large square divided into four equal squares. Take the center vertical line and move it to the left. Now, you still have four boxes, the two boxes on the right, the right column if you will, are larger than the two on the left. Go ahead and denote North, South, East, West, as if you were looking at a map. Psycho and I are sitting in the Southeastern corner, a bedroom. The Northeastern box is another bedroom. The entire Eastern wall of the entire map is a long-ass, walk-in closet that both rooms share. One could enter from either room and exit to the other room if one so desired. The Southwestern box is simply where the stairway leads up to the second floor. The Northwestern box is another closet, making a total of two closets for the Northeastern bedroom – the one that Psycho and I are NOT in. At the intersection of the interior lines of the map is a small landing. While standing on the landing after coming up the stairs, one can turn left to go to the Northeastern bedroom or right to go to the Southwestern bedroom. Again, this is important so stay with me. I am currently leaning against the Southeastern wall, facing west. Behind me is, of course a wall, and on the other side of that wall is the long-ass, walk-in closet. Psycho is sitting near the center of the same bedroom facing me. Back to the story…

Sitting in whispered conversation, Psycho and I were talking about school, track, girls, etc. We were whispering because we could no longer see outside. We had to be quiet in order to ensure our presence would remain undetected. After sitting in darkness for a while, our conversation turned to, "Where the hell is everyone?" And that's when I heard it. A heartbeat. I shit you not.

I repeat, I shit you not. I am not, would not, and will not shit you. I heard an f-ing heartbeat. Psycho heard it, too. My own heart started pounding like it was trying to escape without me. Thank God I didn't have that rare deformity where your heart has two little feet growing out of the bottom of it or, I promise you, my f-ing heart would have tucked artery, sprinted to my asshole, kicked open the door and hauled it's little heart ass all the way back home without me.

"Do you hear that?" I was trying my damndest to whisper but it felt as if I were asking Helen Keller to pass the salt. "Hey, deaf girl! Would you pass the fucking salt? … Please!" That's how loud and awkward my four-word question felt.

Psycho didn't answer. He simply nodded his head. We sat there for at least ten minutes listening to that gawd-awful thump-thump, thump-thump. I tried to stop breathing. I even thought if I could just stop breathing that, maybe, I could make it out of this nightmare alive. Everything I did echoed at what seemed to be a thousand decibels. Swallow – BAM! Blink – BOOM! The subtle turning of my head caused cartilage to explode – RATATATATAT! I prayed I wouldn't tense up and accidentally fart.

Psycho had moved around to face the door, so we were both currently in a position to see anything that approached. The problem was we couldn't see shit. It was so dark that we could faintly tell where the door was as a tiny slit of light was spilling in from the neighboring bedroom.

Finally, the heartbeat faded, and we sat in the thickest fog of silence you can imagine. (I'm about to use the word "suddenly" but I really need you to think about the essence of this word. I'm using it here to mean faster than a pissed-off, greasy lightening bolt could collide with an approaching soaking wet asteroid powered by a tail wind and a super-charged hemi with a bare wire and an open container of rocket fuel – that kind of suddenly.) Suddenly, I saw a silhouette pass by the doorway, moving from the stair landing into the other bedroom. It was the closest I've ever come to shitting myself. In fact, the turd peeked out to see what the commotion was and, seeing the fleeting image of the silhouette, decided it was safer inside. Yes, I was too scared to shit.

Psycho glanced toward me to acknowledge that he, too, had seen the intruder. I could no longer distinguish between the fucking unholy heart beat that started terrorizing us nearly twenty minutes ago and the ridiculous pounding of my own heart that was currently sending a tsunami of blood through my body with each beat.

Psycho leaned over and whispered, "Go see who it is." I looked at him as if he had just asked me to lick his balls. "YOU go see who it is." My ass had suctioned itself to the wood floor, and I wasn't going anywhere.

Psycho nodded and exhaled, "Okay." To my disbelief, he slowly stood and began walking toward the door. He was moving so slowly that he teetered every time he lifted a foot and waited ten or so seconds for the foot to come back down. As Psycho made his way to the middle of the floor, we both heard an additional set of footsteps. Whomever, or whatever, had moved through the other bedroom was now in the large walk-in closet and slowly heading South. The footsteps came closer and closer until they stopped directly behind me. Whatever had joined us was now standing less than two feet away from the back of my head.

Every fiber in my body was screaming at me to dive out the second-story window to my left. I knew that at any moment two large zombie hands would burst through the wall and rip my head off.

A few moments after the footsteps had stopped, Psycho turned back toward the door and continued his stealthy exit. I couldn't believe he was leaving, and I couldn't believe that I couldn't get up and follow. As I watched Psycho disappear through the doorway, I was overcome with dread knowing that only the zombie hands and myself remained.

Accepting the fact that I was surely going to die a gruesome death regardless of my actions, I slowly stood and began the long, precarious journey to the other side of the room. There is neither a desert nor an ocean; indeed, there is no continent on this tiny planet that can equal the expanse of that bedroom that night. After what felt like a lifetime of tiptoeing, floating, and hovering toward the doorway, I arrived just in time to see Psycho climbing out the second-story North window. He motioned for me to quickly follow with an urgency that was in great contrast to our current extreme cautiousness.

In the next one one-hundredth of a second I thought, "Why not take the stairs. We're on the second floor, and I don't know how the hell you're going to get down to the ground if you go out that window. Besides, the stairs are right here. They're safe. Right?" But then, suddenly, someone reached out of the darkness and grabbed for my left leg. I shot about three feet straight up in the air as a hand pounded the wood floor searching for something to latch on to. The instant I hit the ground, I slammed the door at the top of the stairs as hard as I could and sprinted toward Psycho. Out the window, onto the roof, onto the roof of some kind of tool shed or porch, onto the ground and finally, at long f-ing last, we were doing what we did better than any two people in the region – running fast and long without a need or a thought for rest. It's difficult to understand the term "running like your life depends on it" until you have to actually ran like your life depends upon it.

To this day, I can't tell you what was making the heartbeat sound, who was behind the wall, or who was lying on the stairs. I'm sure it wasn't one of my friends because I would have noticed the door stuck to their head that I slammed as I was simultaneously fighting off evil zombie hands and a fear-induced stroke.

As scary as that true story was to live through, it's the following story that continues to haunt me.

When basketball season ended, and I was forced to lace up my track shoes, it was inevitable that Psycho and I were going to endure long workouts of competing against each other. It had been months since everyone began telling me that Psycho could run further and faster than anyone before had even thought about. In fact, even as a sophomore, Psycho began eyeing the school record for the mile and was the first to tell me of a man named Roger Bannister, the first man to break the four minute mile barrier, a goal my fellow track mate was planning to achieve before graduation in just two short years.

A few weeks into training, our track coach, whom had never run further than thirty feet in his entire life, gave Psycho and me an assignment of running ten miles on the track. We often had jaunts of eight to ten miles on the road, which wasn't so bad because the scenery changed and something new was always around the corner. Ten miles on the track was simply torture, an asinine, pointless exercise given as an experiment to see what would happen.

Our forty-lap run began with Psycho pulling away from the start. I had a pretty competitive spirit but running forty laps was more than I could comprehend. I was geared more toward middle distance, like the half mile, so even running a single mile, four laps, was psychologically demanding for me. Forty laps! Who even thinks to ask two kids to run forty laps? Two laps in and Psycho was at least a half-lap ahead of me. He lapped me by the time we had finished two miles. Luckily, I didn't have to endure this humiliation alone. The entire track team was watching me eat dust. Some sad souls even turned their heads as I jogged by, unable to watch my sad, pathetic effort.

By mile eight, Psycho had become bored. A lap-and-a-half ahead of me, he stopped to talk to some members of the girl's track team. Now, don't kid yourself, he wasn't tired. No, indeed, he was feeling great. Psycho had waited for this moment for months. There was no more speculation as to who was the better runner. Not only had he proven that I was nowhere near his league, he was now taking a steamy dump on my pride.

As I approached Psycho and his newly formed entourage, he nodded as if to say, "I'll be with you in a second." I took little comfort in passing him because I was still a full lap behind, a quarter-mile from redemption. I rounded the next two curves of the track and saw that Psycho was still standing in the same spot without a single care that I was moving closer. Now within fifty yards, I watched as he stretched briefly, ended his conversation and leisurely merged back into track traffic.

With the end of our stupid assignment in sight, I was able to summon up enough fortitude to set a new goal – I would try to stay within fifty yards of Psycho. If I could maintain that distance, I would consider it a moral victory.

A strange thing happened on the way to the finish line. Someone started to encourage me. Then another. With a little more than a lap left, I was still within fifty yards. Unlike Psycho, my rhythm had remained constant, though slow, throughout the entire race. Psycho had literally turned off his engine and cooled off. Now, he was virtually starting a second race. Running one long race is very different than running two shorter ones. With one lap left, I was within striking distance as Psycho struggled to get his recovering legs to cooperate. Down to the last two hundred yards, with a mere sixty feet of separation, we were now in my territory and I knew if a long race comes down to a sprint, I can win.

As I crossed the line, I took little consolation in the victory. Despite a few cheers, laughter, and some excitement on an otherwise boring and brain-punching, monotonous day, the simple fact was that Psycho could have easily won. I knew it, and he knew it.

About two weeks later the track season opened in Booneville. Psycho, knowing he could beat me, was aware that his main competition came from J.J. Putter, a little dude from a rival town who was projected to be the year's best. To the surprise of few, Psycho beat J.J. But to the surprise of many, so did I. I sprinted to the finish line, just passing J.J. as Psycho, having already won, turned back to see me clinch second. His eyes widened with genuine excitement, and I could tell he was brother-proud of my accomplishment.

Don't forget this is a terrible story with a tragic ending, both haunting and horrific. If you've enjoyed the buddy aspect of the last few pages and feel satisfied, then you should probably stop reading because this worm is about to turn.

Psycho and I shared a Civics class as well as a Spanish class. One day in Civics, we had a substitute from Zimbabwe. How a Zimbabwean wound up in Ozark, Arkansas must be another tragic story that I hope I never have to hear. However, this was a mellow fellow who was trying to make an impact on some students that he might never see again. He was going around the class asking each student what their dream was. Some answers were as simple as owning a flower shop. Some were ridiculous - Wilson, who had never sang a day in his life, wanted to be a rock star. But one reply was truly thought out and authentic.

Psycho Shawn, a person I had never seen serious a single day that I had known him, stated that he wanted to win a gold medal in the Olympics. He wanted, more than anything, to represent his country by stepping onto the highest platform, and having a gold metal hung around his neck as our National Anthem played. The sincerity of Shawn's deepest wish silenced the room as we all pondered what he was saying. This was a young man with a clear vision of his future. His dream was beyond the city limits of our rural community. It was a big, big dream that, for the briefest of moments, we all visualized. We all saw it in our minds and imaged a fellow student making a global impact. It was a great, distant dream that, for an instant, seemed completely within Shawn's grasp.

Then, suddenly, a dumbass from the back of the room stated, "You better worry about beating Jerry first." Laughter erupted. In a microsecond Shawn's eyes fell to the floor, his face blasted red with uncertainty, and I saw his dream die. The room fell as silent as the night the zombie hands threatened to yank my skull from my head. Each blurt of laughter stomped on Shawn's dream until he felt embarrassment from having imagined such a lofty dream. How silly for a country boy to believe that he could do something beyond baling hay or working for the electric company. The following track meet I beat Shawn, and he never won another race. Over the next few weeks, I witnessed his daring turn to defiance. He no longer trained on weekends or ran with me after school. We were still friends but his focus had clearly been altered. It was as if he had been exposed to a high dose of radiation, and, unlike the movies where the hero becomes invincible, Shawn had been zapped by a lethal injection of peer doubt. Confidence is a funny thing. Much like a fire, it needs to be fed in order to stay hot, alive. Too many icy applications of, "No, you can't", can lead to self-suspicion and the constant speculation that others might be right.

I can't help but wonder what would have become of Shawn had the asshole in the back of Civics class instead shouted, "Give 'em hell, Shawn!" followed by an eruption of applause and twenty classmates chanting, "Psycho! Psycho! Psycho!" At the very least, I would have been lapped at the next track meet as that crazy, running freak would have blown by me with his ass on fire jogging backwards and waving to his fans. But at the most…I really wonder…I'm thinking he could have done it. I truly believe he would have one day become an Olympian. Can we even imagine what great accomplishments we might achieve with something as meager, but constant, as a drip-dose of encouragement?

After my senior year, I was able to arrange a basketball try-out at the University of Central Arkansas. A few weeks prior, Scottie Pippen, who had just left U.C.A and would later win six championships with the Chicago Bulls and enter the National Basketball Hall of Fame, was working out in the stadium as he awaited the start of his first training camp. I had never heard of him but knew that he had just been taken with the fifth draft pick. I sat in the stands with a few other spectators and watched this skinny kid work on his shot. Someone shouted, "Hey, Scottie, can you dunk from the free throw line?" He shrugged his shoulders as if the thought had never occurred to him, "I don't know. Never tried." Palming the ball as effortlessly as if it were a plum, he walked to the half-court line, took a deep breath, and sprinted forward. He planted his big-ass foot on the free throw line and took flight…CLANG! The ball sailed into the air and Scottie nearly fell on his back. At this point, someone could have yelled, "You pussy! Ha! Ha! You nearly busted your ass!" But they didn't. Instead, everyone cheered and begged him to try again. Scottie had tasted blood and now had a goal. He went back to half court with an intense focus and a fierce determination…and I was fortunate enough to witness a tiny bit of basketball history.

I haven't seen Shawn in over fifteen years but I often catch a glimpse of his ghost – a tall, thin, lanky spirit running on a breeze like…no, I have to be honest, it's not a pretty, nor poetic image, just a pissed off ghost. Don't get me wrong here, but I often think his spirit would have been happier had the zombie hands done him in. At least that would have made sense.

BLOODY BUNNY

There are few things Southerner's enjoy more than a good tradition. If you changed the title of "Fiddler on the Roof" to "Coon hunter on a Trailer" you could keep the original theme intact and tell a very similar story. In the South, if you do something once, and someone else thinks its fun…guess what? You've just started a new tradition.

Many years ago, my mom forgot to buy me a Christmas card. She panicked, as any good mother who wants the best for her child would, and began to look for a substitute. While desperately digging through drawers for a left over card from Christ's last birthday, she stumbled across the very card that she had given me the previous year. It was a cute exchange as I noticed last year's entry next to the current year's entry. I have now received that same card for over two decades.

Sometimes putting a special or sentimental twist on tradition can really put a fun jolt in an otherwise predictable holiday routine. When I was about five or six years old, I woke up one Easter morning and peeked out my mobile home window to discover that it had snowed. This type of weather is extremely rare for an Arkansas spring, and in my young mind it meant that something special must be in store for little ol' me. I quickly got dressed and woke up Mom.

Snow, regardless of the time of year, is always special for kids, but on a holiday – it was too good to be true, and I couldn't wait to see what kind of treats waited for me on the crystal covered lawn. It's important to pause here and share my expectations. Easter was like a Christmas primer. There wouldn't be nearly as many gifts, and some of those would be clothes for Easter Sunday church time. The egg hunt, no matter how limited, was always fun. The challenge of out-smarting the bunny that hid them was enough to keep me up the night before planning my pursuit and viewing the landscape in my mind's eye for those tough to sniff out areas of concealment. If I could find every egg it would prove that I, too, was crafty and possessed the natural instincts of a truly wily animal. I was a great hunter of eggs and took to the contest with the zeal of…well… I was really excited.

This next moment must be visualized in slow motion because that's the way I remember it. The mobile home was dark as I was in too much of a hurry to turn on any lights. I raced through the living room with joyful expectations and threw open the plastic and steel door as I felt the bite of cold air and squinted from the blinding sunshine bouncing off the snow covered world. And then… and then, still in slow motion, I glanced down to our tiny 5 foot by 5-foot porch and looked upon a most bizarre twist to a holiday tradition. Not more than two feet away lay a rabbit, whiter than the snow underneath it, surrounded by a half-dozen Easter eggs and the blood from a gunshot wound in its side. "MOM!"

Now, you might think that was a rather disturbing image for a five or six year old boy – and it was. But I find it more interesting that my Uncle had left the little critter there as a way to help me stop believing in the Easter bunny. Indeed, he was trying to help me make a difficult and troublesome realization. I have to admit that it worked. From that point on when people would try to sell me the idea of the Easter bunny, I knew they were full of shit because I saw the bloody bunny dead on my door step, and I can tell you that he ain't comin' back! If you find Easter eggs in your back yard, your parents put them there, not the Easter bunny. I know because I buried the poor bastard.

Eventually, I made a complete psychological recovery and found a way to enjoy the rest of spring. Summer had its usual series of adventures, discoveries, and minor injuries with nothing out of the ordinary to report. Eight months later, on a cold, crisp early morning similar to Bloody Sunday, I stood nervously at the door of our mobile home terrified of what tragedy Christmas morning might have in store.

SHINY HINEY

History has seen many adventurous souls willing to drop trou for a good laugh or to make a bold and necessary statement. Jeffery Chaucer's Canterbury Tales added a raunchy twist with a bearded moon, and I'm certain Mr. Shakespeare must have drawn from at least a few real life experiences in order to become the most famous and respected bawdsman of all. But we cannot award high praise to those who simply wrote about great feats of being bare-assed. The credit, as Mr. Roosevelt once wrote in my favorite piece of literature, "belongs to the man who is actually in the arena, whose face is marred by dust and sweat and blood; who strives valiantly; who errs and comes short again and again; who knows the great enthusiasms, the great devotions, and spends himself in a worthy cause; who, at the best, knows the triumph of high achievement; and who, at the worst, if he fails, at least fails while daring greatly, so that his place shall never be with those cold and timid souls who know neither victory or defeat." You see, to succeed at any art form, especially mooning, you must be willing to risk, to fail, to learn, and to evolve despite the criticism of those around you.

And so it was with my friend Wayne. "Wayne types", to a lesser degree, are common at every high school across the country. He was the guy that never turned down a dare. Hell, most of the time he didn't need a dare, simply the motivation that someone might laugh. He did things like gluing his eyelids to his eyebrows and his upper lip to his nose. He once jumped in an ice-covered river in January just to prove that he would do it. My mom nearly beat him senseless when he ran up and down my street, in the snow, wearing only hiking boots and underwear singing, "Here comes Santa Claus" as loud as he possibly could on the promise of getting one of my Joe Montana rookie cards. And then there's the time he set a teacher's pants on fire with a cigarette lighter during halftime of a football game. (That last one sounds darker than it actually was. In truth, it was the single funniest event to ever happen on earth, and it's a shame there were no cell phone cameras or security cameras rolling to capture a moment of pure comic poetry.)

I could tell you about incidents like Wayne fumigating his testicles with a can of bug spray because he had a bad chigger infestation. I could tell you about the speed and precision with which he could execute a perfect wedgie and escape unseen. There are countless stories I could tell but I dare not run the risk of skewing this story or creating a false image of my friend.

One of my earliest memories of Wayne involves my acceptance by the cool kids. In the seventh grade, I was a loner. Not necessarily an outcast, just a loner. One day, in the boy's bathroom, I got into in argument with Wilson, Wayne's best friend and the natural athlete of my class who was the poster boy for the 80's preppie movement with his curling-ironed hair, pink Izod, and ultra-white Nikes. We were smack-talking, which was a specialty of mine, and Wilson was getting more and more frustrated because people were gathering and, as far as wit-sparring goes, he had brought the equivalent of a balloon sword to gunfight.

I had just tossed a stinging retort back to Wilson that brought laughter and "ooohs!" from the crowd. (I would give my left nut to remember this exchange. If anyone remembers it, write it down, send it to me, and I will mail you my left nut.) Wilson was down to his final five words. His vocabulary and imagination were spent on, "I know you are but what am I." With a dry mental tank and the onlooker's expectations growing, Wilson took a menacing step forward. "Do you want to fight?" Silence. It couldn't have been quiet for more than a few seconds but the intensity was as thick as the front of Wilson's skull. Finally, Wayne casually tossed out, "Kick his ass, McNutt." Wilson was shocked and looked up at Wayne as if they had just broken up. He gathered what strength he had left and gave me the old, "You're not worth it" line straight out of Red Dawn. Just like that, the commotion had ended and Wayne and I were friends.

The undisputable tie that bound Wayne and I was basketball. In a small town, being a good athlete is crucial to achieving any subsequent goals one may have in life, if any other success is actually needed. During my eighth grade summer, I moved from the backwoods back into town. Wayne and I spent the entire summer together and every single day, despite sizzling heat or pouring rain, involved hours of playing ball. It didn't take long until we dominated Eastside Park's chain-netted hoops and defeated anyone who dared step on our asphalt court.

One day, early in our junior year, the basketball team was warming up for practice. Pre-practice was goof-off time as everyone tried to relax and get loose before a tough, demeaning, physically demanding training session. This was also the time of day when the cheerleaders arrived in the gym to start their own practice. You know those cheerleaders that you see in movies that train and train and come up with all kinds of athletic moves and dance their asses off to super cool music while getting the crowd fired up in a dramatic display of team spirit. Well, that really wasn't these gals. Wayne and I decided to throw a little excitement into their workout routine of combing hair, giggling, and gossiping. Becky came waltzing in with an armload of books, completely expecting this day to be exactly like the previous day, and, indeed it was, until she heard her name shouted over the sound of a dozen bouncing balls and the rapid squeaking of sneakers. She turned her eighties-permed head to the right and saw something that completely terrified her – Wayne and I were standing at half court, bent over, with our bare, naked asses staring at Becky's innocent eyes. Her scream shocked everyone in the gym. She dropped her books and, I swear, nearly fainted. But that scream! It was so loud and so full of horror and despair. To this day, I've never heard anything so desperate, so hopeless.

This continued every school day for the next three or four weeks. Becky entered the gym unaware, heard her name, screamed bloody murder, nearly fainted and dropped her books while everyone laughed. Eventually, the gag got old so we started mooning other cheerleaders who all had similar reactions.

But like any drug, the need to go bigger eventually took over. Before long, Wayne and I were creating mooning rules like, the victim, or target as we referred to them, must be completely unaware that the moon is coming; if they even see you bend over, the moon is out of bounds and cannot count for the weekly total. We even gave our best moons names like Peek-a-boo moon, Ninja moon, Cherry-bomb moon, Half-moon, Single cheeker, Bat cave, Mud puddle, Dental floss and the Drive-by. We even invented new ways to moon multiple people, of which two examples are forthcoming.

Wayne and I quickly developed a reputation as hooligan mooners. As the stakes grew higher, the difference in our skill levels and determination became apparent. One night we were planning a routine Ghost Buster. This particular maneuver requires a dark setting and large objects to hide behind. As Mandy and Erin, a cheerleader and her best friend, walked out of the house, across the dark driveway, Wayne and I made a subtle but strange noise, similar to the gurgle of a water cooler, to get their attention. As they glanced toward the trees we were hiding behind, we shuffled out into view, asses bare, hands and feet on the ground. If the conditions are dark enough, the victims can only see, what appears to be, detached rumps floating in the air. Both girls screamed bloody murder and jumped into the other's arms. Wayne and I pulled up our pants and bolted into the night.

Moments later, we were jogging down the street, laughing at our success, when we heard an engine roar to life and suddenly realized we were being chased. We raced hard to get to the end of the block, so we could turn the corner and hide. The car zoomed forward and suddenly we were sprinting, fully illuminated, in its headlights. I looked to my right and Wayne was gone. He must have dove over a fence, risking trespassing over failure. Before I knew it, the car was right beside me. Knowing I couldn't get away, I stopped, exhausted from the run and breathless from fear.

The window rolled down and laughter spilled out of the car. To my shock, it wasn't Mandy and Erin. It was Mandy's mom, a school administrator, and Ms. Greylene, the Phys. Ed. coach and neighbor of Mandy. The two women had been talking, unbeknownst to Wayne and I, in a nearby yard. They witnessed the whole event. Both were laughing hysterically, barely able to breath. Finally, Mandy's mom blurted out, "You've got the whitest ass I've ever seen!"

They say criminals never see the end coming. Arrogance leads to sloppiness and sloppiness leads to defeat. I stood underneath the streetlight in the cold air, humiliated, naked beneath my clothes, fully exposed on the outside. I had been busted by two off duty teachers, who were laughing at me not with me.

The following weekend, Wayne tried to get my confidence up by concocting a new mooning scheme. The Sonic had a driveway that circled the entire building. At the end of the turn, there was a tall fence that blocked access to a small hillside. Not far from that fence was another taller fence. The plan was to sneak between the two fences, drop trou, leap up and grab the top of the second fence and hold on tight. As cars rounded the corner, their headlights would illuminate a wall of naked asses.

We had a few new recruits that night as we jogged into place. I was still feeling the embarrassment of our previous exploit and couldn't focus on the mission – I was off my game. I didn't see a large, three-inch thick cable sticking out of the ground. I hit it hard, tearing my shirt as well as a ripping a gash across my rib cage. "Go on without me!" I lay on the ground clutching my wound as the others hunkered down, moving quickly through the dense grass. A few moments later, as I limped back alone in the dark, I heard laughter and car horns signifying another victory for Wayne, another defeat for me.

I soon began coming up with excuses to not go mooning as Wayne's legend grew and grew. Before long, being mooned by Wayne had become a point of pride, an exclusive club whose members were linked by brief moments of confusion, then laughter.

Wayne soon became haunted by the pressure of when to retire, just as all great professional athletes do. When was enough truly enough? High school seniors loved Wayne and began challenging him to take on greater and riskier stunts. Finally, one night in mid-January, it all came crashing down.

Our basketball team had finished with the best regular season record in the conference and the town was buzzing about the forthcoming district tournament. Subiaco, a boy's academy, was our biggest rival. Looking for any edge we could find, the team went to their final home game to scout for weaknesses in our soon-to-be opponent.

On the way back, Wayne was riding with some seniors. I was riding with a couple of other teammates. As Wayne's car sped down the highway, they noticed Coach Graft up ahead. A dare to moon the coach was soon issued, the windows were rolled down and the gas petal stomped. As Wayne and the boys pulled along side Coach Graft, they honked and flashed their lights to add to the spectacle.

Coach Graft was typically a very stoic man, always careful to keep distance between he and his players as to not compromise his authority. He had a subtle sense of humor that often landed with lots of laughter from his players. If the joking got too out of hand, he would shake his head and walk away. Everyone thought an innocent moon would be well received. After all, we had just finished a long season and were poised to be district champions. But there was one thing that no one in Wayne's car was aware of.

Wayne's ass moved into position, filling the frame of the passenger side window just as the two vehicles aligned. Coach Graft looked to his left and must have known instantly whose butt he was staring at. With no outward sign of the internal anger, his eyes turned back to the highway. "Did you see that?" He asked matter-of-factly. "Yes, daddy, but I turned my head." replied his twelve-year-old daughter.

A sin had been committed. A stray moon had hit an innocent victim and her honor had to be restored. This poor little girl's life would forever change. She was now aware that boys had butts. I shudder to think what her life has now become due to nothing more than rotten timing.

As for Wayne, he was kicked off the basketball team. His girlfriend, unable to handle this final humiliation, broke up with him while urging him to seek help; first from the Lord, then from a professional. My best friend's world was collapsing around him. Would the legend go down defeated and stripped of his honor? The entire town was quickly made aware that one of their star players had been suspended for conduct unbecoming to the team. Wherever Wayne went, people would stare, point, and ask why or how could you?

As time expired during the championship game, our hard-fought victory was most difficult to celebrate. I don't remember the clapping, high-fiving, trophies or cheerleaders. The only image I remember from winning the district title is Wayne standing in the corridor wearing street clothes, not knowing what to do, wanting to come onto the floor where only players were allowed.

Eventually, the awkwardness of Wayne's suspension wore away and he was quickly accepted back into the fold. We spent the entire summer hiking, camping, biking, and playing basketball. When school started again, we were in tip-top shape. We were seniors and our team took to the hardwood floors dominating the entire season. We easily marched onward to win our second consecutive district championship. For this celebration, Wayne stood in the thick of an elated team with an excited town cheering in the stands.

What happened to the legend; the mooning champ of Ozark high? Did Coach Graft finally get through to the boy and tame his wild side with the firm hand of discipline? Was the punishment of suspension validated by our title defense? It had been over a year since any major mooning had occurred. Perhaps the champ had lost his touch, his edge worn dull.

On the last day of school, Wayne told me to spread the word that something was going to happen in the main yard between the cafeteria and the gym. By the time the bell rang for lunch, everyone was eager to gather for something to break the monotony of the longest, most pointless day of the year. Twenty minutes into the lunch break and we were baking in the hot sun. Hunger and boredom began to do battle when, without warning, someone pointed toward the announcer's booth in the gym. Through the large glass window at the top of the basketball gym, in a room that was supposed to be locked, stood Wayne with his arms out and a wicked grin that gleamed of both confidence and conquest. Sixty feet up, with no intent to hide his identity, he turned his back to an anxious audience and the most famous full moon of all shone brighter than a noon sun in June. Cheers erupted from the courtyard crowd as lunch duty teachers raced in vain to the gym. Of course, by the time those in pursuit hit the gym doors, he was gone, replaced by a legend. There were close to four hundred witnesses who saw nothing. The teachers only looked in time to see the offense take place, a faceless ass with no identifying marks. It was a mass moon and the authorities were left with their pants down, defeated.

The victor from all wars waged is simply defined as the last man laughing.

In one brave move, Wayne had reclaimed the campus, the basketball gym, and his rightful place in the Class Clown Hall of Fame.

What, you might ask, was his curtain call? One hour after escaping the gym, with teachers still interrogating freshman about the dastardly deed that had just taken place, Wayne streaked across the entire campus wearing only a pair of white Pumas with green stripes while shouting the theme music to Indiana Jones through his own laughter. He dove in a getaway car waiting on the corner of 13rd and School Street, and to the best of my knowledge, has never set foot on campus again.

And that, folks, is how you go out on top.

DROOPSY

After the eighth grade ended, Mom and step-dad decided to leave the country. By country I mean a sparsely populated area with lots of hills, trees, and critters. Selling the mobile home turned out to be more of a problem than anyone had anticipated. Finding a buyer was the easy part. But for the first time in many years, moving meant packing and countless trips back and forth across the river bridge with a pickup truck full of boxes and furniture.

About half way through our move a classmate rode by on a bike and asked if we needed any help. From that moment on, Wayne and I were best friends. After talking my mom into buying a bike for me, Wayne and I spent the next three months pedaling across every square inch of town and often beyond city limits. The only time we got off our bikes was to hike or play basketball. As it turned out, hundreds of miles of biking had an interesting side effect.

When summer had ended, I discovered that I was suddenly much faster than I was the previous spring. I still wasn't as fast as Wilson but I could damn near run the entire day. I was also closer to my ultimate goal of dunking a basketball. I could dunk a volleyball, which had absolutely no practical use whatsoever and only emphasized the fact that I couldn't quite dunk a basketball. However, it was much better than having to suffer the degrading dunking of a tennis ball which was akin to being seen riding through town on a Moped that was purchased from a girl who was too embarrassed to be seen on it – but that's another story.

Basketball season offered its comforting and predictable disappointments of underachieving and folding under the pressure of a screaming, frustrated coach begging to see the potential he swore I might have. In striking contrast, track season yielded something I was completely unaccustomed to…success. I wasn't fast enough to run with the sprinters and simply didn't care to run the two-mile event but the half-mile, for whatever reason, was a perfect fit. Don't get me wrong, I hated track. This dying sport garnered no support, but it did provide me with something to do after basketball season. This year, however, had a new ingredient. I was winning.

I have to admit that I have a certain degree of respect for those that run track but never win. It's such an agonizing sport that demands maximum effort and guarantees nothing more than muscle cramps and a constant mind scramble. I approached each race with dread and hesitation that lingered right up to the explosion of that damn starter's pistol. Bang! I bolted forward and instantly felt out of breath. I only had to run a total of two laps and halfway through the first lap I always felt my legs thicken and my lungs begin to seize as if I were inhaling hot smoke. By the end of every first lap I would convince myself that second place was totally acceptable. (Begin inner monologue of ever half-mile I've every competed in.) Hell, even if I came in third, my coach should still be happy. Third place isn't really all that bad considering there are usually between twelve and fifteen athletes competing and only the top six are awarded points. Yeah, third place will be just fine. After all, I train like a mad man so I shouldn't feel the least bit disappointed about third place.

Why is everyone looking at me? What are you looking at? Who said that? Of course I know there's less than a lap remaining! What an idiot! There are only two laps total. Do they actually think I didn't notice that I just completed the first lap? Oh, great, side stitches. There's got to be some cure for this. Why does my side do this every race? Is it my ribs reacting to the sudden increase in breathes per minute? Okay, let's see…two breaths in, one breath out. Two breaths in, one breath out. I bet no one else knows about my secret breathing pattern. Suckers! Wow, Crowley's taking a nice lead. Probably thinks I'll be coming soon. Well, good for him. He'll get his first win. I could probably catch Perkins if I wanted to. I don't want to. I'm comfortable with third. Very comfortable with third. Why are they yelling at me to go? If I had a little extra air capacity I could scream out, "Relax, I'm going for third!" That would sound weird. Going for third. I suppose it's not very ambitious.

Maybe I could just hold up three fingers. But that would look like I was boasting. Who brags about third? Screw it. Sorry Perkins, you're just too tempting. I'll lengthen my stride a little and…there we go. Yeah, second place feels much better. I wonder…Crowley is only about twenty yards ahead with half a lap to go. I don't know. Second is good. Second is good. Lots of points for second place. Why is every one screaming at me? Second is good! I'm totally fine with second place. But…I'm right here, well within striking distance. He's in the last curve. I better go now. A little more on the stride. That's right you little bastard, I'm moving up. You know I'm coming don't you? You better know it. Okay, let's get those arms swinging. Faster with the arms, so I don't have to think about the legs so much. Man, I love running the final curve. Get a nice little lean going to the inside. Coach is looking at his watch and waving me on. I wonder if I'm close to my best time. That would be cool. Nice curve, only ten yards back. Focus on the finish line. Slide out to the right. Fuck, I'm not going to make it. Damn it! Bullshit, I'll make it. He's feeling me. That's right, buddy, they're not cheering for you, they're warning you. "He's coming! He's gaining on you!" Yes, he is. Shoulder to shoulder with fifteen yards to go and you already know you've lost. See ya later.

And so it was for every track meet for the entire season. Dread, pain, doubt, acceptance, denial, surge, surge, win, cramps. Track cramps are different than regular cramps. I've actually had a hamstring snap tight so violently that it jerked me out bed and sent me flopping around on the floor like a catfish on asphalt in July.

The last race of the year, the district meet had a new challenge for me to loathe. In addition to my regular events, I was asked to compete in the high jump.

My coaches were hoping that if I could simply place I would get a few unexpected points that would give our team an edge for the over all title. At the time, we didn't have anyone competing in the event so any warm body was certainly an improvement. Besides, it's not a grueling endurance event so what's the worst that could happen?

I had about three days to train and needed to clear 5'4" to qualify. I had enough of a vertical jump to make one think that I would be a natural at the high jump. However, there's absolutely nothing natural about the high jump. It's a completely awkward and foreign contortion for the body to perform at a full sprint. Imagine running toward an object, jumping off your outside foot, turning sideways so that the object is no longer in your sight, throwing your arms up and behind you so that your back arches in a an uncomfortable half circle. Now, at the height of your jump, you are almost completely horizontal. Head and shoulders are a breeze, it's the ass and legs that get you in trouble. Simply flex your stomach as hard as you possibly can the instant your ass clears the bar and whip those legs up fast. If you do everything right, you'll land on your shoulders and then do some type of awkward flip as your neck nearly snaps in half. If you do anything wrong, you'll probably have the same results with the addition of a metal bar slammed against your spine. What a stupid event!

When the district track meet finally rolled around, I privately hoped for a rain out. As all of the high jump participates were warming up, an odd phenomenon began to occur – athletes were missing the mat. Every high jump bar has a line denoting its center point, which serves as a guideline to those approaching take off. I was the least experienced jumper and for the life of me I couldn't understand how anyone with an ounce of intelligence could completely miss a 10' x 10' x 3' bright blue mat sitting in full sunlight at the end of freshly laid blacktop runway on a rich, green field. My confidence began to soar.

The jumper in front of me, to my surprise, also missed the f-ing mat. The rest of us snickered at the poor, embarrassed dumb ass. I can't remember the joke that was cracked as I began my sprint, but I know it was funny as hell. As a matter of fact, it was so funny that I was laughing during my approach. I always believed that laughter contained healing powers, which meant that it was a positive life force, and, therefore, could only enhance my performance rather than distract or diminish it. My track spikes dug deep into the tarmac-like surface as I gained speed with each step of my twelve-stride sprint. With my right foot planted firmly, I swooped down, pulling inward to prepare for liftoff.

Still smiling, my right knee thrust upward without causing any decrease in velocity and my arms drove hard toward the sky as my back arched over the bar. "Damn, that felt great!" To this point, it was my most perfect jump – and I was still grinning. "Flex the abs and get those legs up!" Could it really be this easy? Well, for a few physically gifted individuals, I suppose so. Now to stick the landing – with a smile. I tilted my head slightly to the right to check my airborne position and thought, "What's that? What the hell is that? Hmmm. I guess the top of the mat is black. Odd, I would have guessed it would be blue like the rest of the mat. Oh, wait a minute…" My smile faded. "That's not the mat… it's...asphalt." Bam! Lights out. Silence.

No one saw the alligator rush on to the field. Due to the fact that it was wearing Bermuda shorts and a Panama Jack tee-shirt, it cleverly blended in with the parents and random sports enthusiasts. The reptilian spoilsport had its Walkman blasting so loudly that I could hear it from the second deck of my speedboat. He was a brash, young croc full of angst and a bold determination to prove himself in front of so many detractors. He tore off his disguise like Clark Kent becoming Superman to reveal a Spandex bodysuit stretched across his ripped and scaly frame. He arrogantly laughed in my direction as I defiantly raised my middle finger. The race was on!

I'm pretty sure I was only unconscious for a second or two, which is understandable considering the head trauma caused by jumping as high as you possibly can only to land on your noggin. "My shoulder hurts." As the strangers with concerned faces helped me to my feet, I saw their worry turn to disturbed confusion. "No, my head is fine. Actually, my shoulder is killing me. Ow."

I was instructed to go see my coach for a check up. As I walked through the bleachers to make my way toward our camp, I couldn't help but notice that everyone I passed looked at my bruised jaw, then to my shoulder, then all the way down to the fingers of my right hand. Curiosity finally got the best of me so I glanced down to my own fingers which seemed to be just fine, expect for the fact that they were about five inches lower then where I was used to seeing them.

Imagine standing upright and being able to scratch your kneecaps without bending over. Apparently, when a collarbone breaks, there's nothing to support the arm, and the shoulder can sag a considerable, albeit painful, distance. Now that I was completely aware of the injury, I was suddenly equally aware of the severe throbbing taking place in the area where my two right collars bones used to be connected into one longer, stable bone. "Ooowww!"

Coach looked me over for a few minutes. He was taking his time and using great caution as to not misdiagnose my situation. After all, he was a coach, not a doctor, and he was well aware of his responsibility to care for his athletes regardless of the outcome of any menial sporting event. His trained eyes darted back and forth from my left shoulder to my right as he evaluated the severity of injury.

"You've got the droopsy."

"The droopsy?"

He crossed his arms as he confirmed his diagnoses. "Yep. It's the droopsy. When you landed on your shoulder you stretched all those muscles. Don't worry. They'll snap back into shape in a day or so. You'll be fine."

"Can I run?"

His moustache began to twitch. It was the kind of question that coaches have nightmares about. The more his wheels began to turn, the more concerned I became about his answer. If he said no, a part of me would be thrilled. I hated running and could never come up with a satisfactory answer as to why I ever signed up for such a torturous and meaningless extra curricular activity. If he would just say no I could rest, or go eat my Carl Buddig ham-like sandwich and drink my peach Nehi, or, at the very least, continue moaning about the pain until I got some sympathy from the girls track team.

But…if he said no…there was a down side. Our camp was only about ten yards from the track. I began to imagine myself sitting on the side watching some dude I've been beating all year win my event and get my shiny blue ribbon with gold lettering. It was so shiny…

"I can run."

"Are you sure? That droopsy might get a little aggravated with all the bouncing around. But…if you're sure."

He was right. A half-mile of bouncing around did aggravate my droopsy. Even though I ran with my right arm tucked close to my body, it only took me a few strides to realize what a stupid, incredibly painful, decision I had made. The good news is that my really long, ritualistic, only-to-be-used-while-running inner-monologue was replaced with a simple chat consisting of two words: Ow and shit.

"Ow. Shit. Ow. Shit. Ow. Shit. Ow. Shit. Ow. Shit. Ow. Shit. Ow. Shit. Ow. Shit. Ow. Shit. Shit. Shit. Ow. Shit. Ow. Shit. Ow. Shit. Ow…Ow.

About halfway through the race, people started to stare, not at the race, but at the moronic kid with a saggy shoulder. My teammates cheered and offered encouragement as I went by. I suddenly realized that no one was watching the race. They were watching me.

Everyone knows that Clorox and Draino can be a volatile combination. The same can be said for peer pressure and social shame. The realization that second place was not going to be acceptable propelled me to stay at the head of the pack. The problem with social shame is that it behaves more like shotgun pellets than a bullet – it has a wide pattern of influence. More specifically, the guy behind me was feeling the pressure of being beaten by a gimp, which, of course, escalated his desire to be at the front of the pack. I can only guess that the runner in third place was abso-freaking-lutely comfortable with prospect of an anonymous white ribbon.

I sloshed back and forth grunting and struggling for what must have been the ugliest, most pathetic, down-right saddest looking win in the history of track. By the time I was making my way down the final stretch, most people had simply covered their eyes, unable to stomach the pitiful spectacle. It was kinda like watching the next-to-last-of-the-Mohicans go down in that Daniel Day-Lewis film. Remember the guy that fights the bad-ass Crow played by Wes Studi? The next-to-the-last-Mohican gets his arm sliced, a rib shattered, and his lung pierced but he just keeps coming back for more. Every time I watch that movie I keep hoping Burgess Meredith will pop his head out of the bushes and yell, "Stay down, kid! Stay down!"

The euphoria of winning the half-mile lasted about seven and a half minutes. The throbbing returned to my shoulder and the droopsy intensified. The bus ride home was bumpy, and, a few hours later, the constant motion of my waterbed proved to be a new chapter in self-prescribed torture. Saturday was even worse, and by Sunday morning I was a cranky, pissed-off, whiny, irritable pain in the ass. By Sunday night, mom had had enough and insisted that I go to the doctor the following day – after school, of course.

Since I was a relatively fast healer and never missed school due to illness, I had no reservations about the doctor's appointment. What's the worst that could happen? I figured I'd probably have to put a salve on the injury or maybe take some gnarly tasting medicine. When I was told I would have to get an x-ray, I was actually excited. This was could be fun.

The diagnosis was determined about five seconds after the x-ray came back. It was clear that a bone was broken and that "droopsy" may have been an understatement. As I looked at the black and white image of my upper skeletal system I couldn't help but notice a golf-ball like shape that was centered perfectly over the fracture. I had been curious about this for a few days since it had been clearly visible about an hour after the accident. I had assumed the lumps were simply swelling due to trauma, like when Sylvester the Cat gets clubbed with a frying pan and a giant knot protrudes from the top of his skull. I was wrong.

When a bone breaks, the area is instantly flooded with calcium to repair the damage. It's a lot like a quick and dirty spackle job. It's quick because it happens right away and dirty because so much of the mending substance floods the area. In the first few hours, the calcium deposit is somewhat flexible allowing for a short window of time to set the bone at the correct angle. However, if one doesn't seek immediate help and waits, oh, let's say three days before seeing a doctor, then that little freaking knot of new bone becomes as solid as any other bone – only it's set at the wrong angle.

There was a twinge in the Doctor's face for a split second. "We'll have to reset it."

"What does that mean", I asked?

"Ah…hmmm. Let me get a nurse. You just wait right here. This only takes a few seconds. She'll be right with you."

He left the room with such a hurried and awkward bolt that I couldn't tell if he had just farted or was trying to escape an uncomfortable situation. I sat shirtless and alone in the cold room pondering what "reset" could possibly mean. Nothing came to mind. The best I could come up with was some type of cast "set" on my shoulder to "repair" the damage. I always wanted a cast. Every kid I ever knew who had a cast received tons of attention and had all those fun autographs and funny pictures drawn on it. I thought, "Yeah, that'll be fun. Let's do that."

I startled as the door flew open, and I turned to see what I thought was a celebrity. For a brief moment, I mistook the bulky figure in white for an actress who played a character named Buella Ballbreaker from the movie Porky's. Buella was the school nurse and bore an uncanny resemblance to comic Jonathan Winters. Admittedly, this would have been a minor celebrity, but still, the nurse in front of me looked familiar. I can't say for certain, but as best I remember, her entrance was also paired with a clap of lightening, the sudden bawl of old organ, and maybe, again I can't say for certain, but I thought I heard a wolf howl. I am certain that the fluorescent lights flickered followed by a fifteen-degree drop in temperature.

She tossed my file onto a nearby counter and came to a stop directly in front of me. For a moment, she seemed offended by my injury. Her squinty stare and flexed jaw reminded me of the German Sheppard that bit me in the ass when I was twelve years old. I slowly leaned back as she leaned in and continued her intense examination. Finally, she grunted some type of assurance to herself and looked me in eye as if to weigh my courage. At this moment she and I suffered a significant miscommunication. Big Nurse nodded as if we were in agreement but my expression should have conveyed fear or, at the very least, confused panic. I'm not sure what I did wrong. Perhaps it was because I didn't say anything. I was actually hoping my silence would cause her to become bored and leave the room at which point I could climb out of a window or hide in the trash until the Wednesday morning pickup.

Big Nurse grabbed a step stool and walked around the table behind me. I was too afraid to look over my shoulder for fear of seeing an instrument that might escalate my current unease. The table shook as she climbed up and wobbled within inches of my bare back. Her ice cold hands were like iron clamps, her arm went around the front of my neck as if she were taking me hostage in a police standoff, her right arm slid under my right arm with her elbow in my armpit and her hand curling back to her own shoulder. My instinct was to scream for help, but the sheer terror of being so tightly constricted caused me to go into some sort of trance. I suddenly understood why the wild boar relaxes as the anaconda flexes.

She rocked me slightly to the left as she shifted her weight and drove her knee into my spine. With three solid points of contact, Big Nurse had rendered me as powerless as a wet pasta puppet. She took a deep breath and steadied herself as an eerie calm settled over the room. It was like every horror movie you've ever seen when the victims have that split-second where they think that maybe, just maybe, they're going to survive only to have some sort of bloody, mangled mess of a creature appear inches away, teeth bared and eyes wide, just as the sound track explodes and the audience releases a collective dump in the their red velvet chair. It was so like that.

Big Nurse slowly exhaled as she slowly said, "This… will…hurt."

Her knee thrust forward like a switchblade as she jerked her arms back. I wasn't sure what I had done to piss this lady off but it must have been bad. After the initial recoil, we were both leaning forward again. Still not having the time to scream, she snapped me back, harder and further than before.

"What the…owww! You crazy fu – owww! Oh, god, please send your son to destroy this evil bi-oww!" It's so hard to get a good curse going when someone is trying to rip your head off.

She yanked again. I could tell she was getting angry that whatever was supposed to happen during this complicated medical procedure was clearly taking too long.

The razor-sharp pain in my shoulder began to subside, replaced by a euphoric dullness that washed across my body. I can only guess that my soul sensed it would be moving on and was telling the body good-bye. My eyes rolled up but didn't have the momentum to stay, so they kept looping to the outside and falling back down again.

I was only about four or five seconds into the attack at this point and suddenly the entire event became hilarious. My eyes were wandering in all directions, and I could no longer hold my head up. I began laughing uncontrollably as I visualized myself being dishonored by a middle-aged, overweight, hyper-aggressive, mistress of distress. My jaw fell open as drool spilled out. A snot bubble swelled and exploded. I began a mental countdown of when the floodgates of my bowels would break open. Under normal circumstances, I would focus all of my efforts to keep from soiling myself. However, this nut of a nurse deserved to be shat upon, and only a few seconds remained before I initiated my unholy revenge.

Three…two…SNAP! Aaaaaah! Silence.

I can't say for sure if I was breathing or not, but I know I was alive. I had lived. No movement was possible as I slipped in and out of a shock-induced coma. Big Nurse slapped her hands together with the energy and enthusiasm of celebrating a job well done.

"There we go. That was a lot of calcium buildup you had there. Wasn't sure if I could break it or not."

I summoned up all the strength I could muster and tapped "Fuck you" in Morris code on the cold metal table. Confused, my soul hovered above me for a few minutes, not knowing whether or not it should stay on earth or ascend to a safer place. Finally, it floated back down and looked me in the eye as if to say, "We can end this." At last, my soul shook his head, annoyed by having to stay on this violent planet any longer, and slipped back inside me.

Luckily, the numbness from such a brutal assault allowed me to remain comfortable in my vegetative state as I was fitted for a harness that would hold my newly fractured collarbone in its proper position until it was healed.

Yank, zip, jerk, pull, push, twist, stretch. "How's that Mr. McNutt? Is that comfortable?"

"Who?" My eyes crossed so hard that I could see my cerebral cortex.

She leaned her fat head further into my distorted vision, "Your harness. Is it comfortable?"

I nodded, acknowledging the misunderstanding, "I like biscuits."

Two weeks later, still wearing the padded harness, I decided to go for a bike ride. I had mastered riding with no hands years earlier so having one good limb to rely on should be plenty. I was crossing the street in front of the Magic Burger and was heading towards town. Halfway across the street, I realized there was no ramp, only a curb.

"Shit."

Reaching quickly for the hand break, I knocked the front wheel sideways. This probably wouldn't have been a big deal if not for the sand. The wheel whipped perpendicular to the bike and instantly stopped moving. The bike, unlike the front wheel, continued moving in an arching motion, rotating up and over the wheel. As I flew forward, I instinctively reached out with both hands to catch myself. It was the third collarbone break in less than three weeks.

My bike and I, both injured and embarrassed, sat on the curb brainstorming what we would tell mom. She would have one of two reactions: anger or concern. With the current circumstances, it was a coin flip at best. What kind of idiot gets on a bike with a broken collarbone? My bike pointed out that I would be forcing mom to decide between paying for a doctor's visit or roast beef with potatoes. It was a valid point. I gave a tug on the harness strap to tighten it just a bit. There was no way in hell I was going back to the doctor and passing on roast beef made even less sense. Who gives a crap if my right arm is a little longer than my left? After all, a feller's got to eat and a little droopsy never hurt anybody.

LUCKY NUMBER THIRTEEN

Since I was raised by a single mom, my maternal grandparents were an ever-present influence in my life. We visited the grandfolk practically every weekend and, despite the long drive, I always enjoyed spending time with Grandpa and Grandma. Summertime allowed longer visits, and I would often stay a week at a time. Grandpa was in his 70's but still maintained an enormous garden that covered three sides of his home. His crop included corn, pumpkins, okra, tomatoes, snap beans, watermelon, and potatoes. Although the pumpkin and watermelon patch offered what I considered to be the coolest plants, it was the corn that served a greater purpose. An extended visit with anyone, no matter how much you love them, can become tedious and sometimes even a young boy needs a break. Since there was no cave system or mountain within walking distance, a large forest of corn was a respectable substitute. With the effort of five walking strides, I could easily vanish and remain hidden as long as needed. Since my grandparents place was where I made countless discoveries, a place of seclusion was a sanctuary for the imagination. The cornfield provided the security I needed to slowly turn the pages of the bra and panty section of the Sears catalogue. This was, of course, an experiment that raised many more questions than it answered. (Many of those countless questions would be answered the following summer while snooping around in Grandpa's room and discovering a different magazine hidden under the mattress.)

My second favorite place to hide was my grandfather's closet. It was a small closet but I was still a small boy so space wasn't an issue. I remember sneaking in an emergency flashlight and a small wooden box out of the lower left drawer of his dresser and bolting to the closet with what I considered to be the most sacred items the world had ever known.

Once inside the closet, I would carefully, stealthily, climb to the top of a pile of boxes and slide the flannel shirt collection to completely conceal my presence. Even if someone opened the door to look for me, it would seem illogical that I could be there upon first glance. I was smart enough to not push my luck and never stayed in the closet for more than five or ten minutes. The area was so small and quite that the sound of my breathing took on an ominous quality as the flannel kept out fresh oxygen and retained every kilowatt of body heat. The flashlight clicked on and was propped in a corner. I always opened the display box as if I were an archeologist in an Egyptian tomb on the brink of a great discovery. War medals weren't to be taken lightly. As young as I was, I knew they were earned through unspeakable sacrifice. Two of the awards were given during World War II. The remaining six were from Vietnam and were awarded the same year I was born.

Stepping out of Grandpa's closet and turning right, the next room was an enclosed back porch. My family referred to it as a sleeping porch. I later learned that this term was unique to the Nixon's. Since there was a total of ten children, there was a bed in every room of the house, the majority of the beds were on the sleeping porch. All of the kids were adults now but one bed still remained so the term sleeping porch was as appropriate as ever. The sleeping porch was now a sort of guest room. During the hot, humid summers it was the best room in a house without air conditioning. With all of the widows open, and a box fan sitting on a kitchen chair not more than two feet away, my sleep was always deep and, more often than not, late.

On the other side of the sleeping porch was a large freezer. Freezers of this type are common in the South as many people raise some type of livestock and a large freezer is necessary to keep large quantities of meat from spoiling. Hanging just above the freezer was a family portrait. It was the last portrait ever taken of the entire Nixon family, but in truth, it was about one week too late.

Most family portraits are littered with smiles and artificially generated poses and awkward tilts of the head. This picture was hauntingly honest. Only a few of the twelve individuals are smiling and most aren't even looking at the camera. They seem incapable of hearing the photographer's countdown through the fog of emotion that so heavily hangs about them. But the most noticeable family member is the one who wasn't even present when the shutter blinked and the film absorbed the second darkest moment of my family's challenging history.

In the upper right-hand corner of the second row of Nixon's, was Sammie. Out of focus, fading, and outlined by awkward bending edges, the second oldest son was a cut-out of a previous picture inserted about one week after the group photo was taken, about one week after he was buried. Sammie was killed in Vietnam. He died a hero but I won't go into the details because all that matters when a loved one dies is dealing with the pain of their absence.

Dale, the oldest brother of the family and best friend to Sammie, stood defiantly centered in the picture. He was the one who insisted on the portrait when no else could tolerate the idea of a gathering minus one. Dale had come home to bury Sammie and take care of business before returning to the war. He took out an insurance policy and tried to spend some quality time with each family member.

Gene, sitting in the front row, had just arrived from front line combat and was sitting next to Jerry, who had flown in from Boot Camp training. My grandmother and grandfather sat in the middle of the front row. Grandpa looked at the floor while Grandma looked in the direction of the camera but miles beyond it. Barbara, Mary, Fannie Mae, Glenda, and Kay all made attempts to smile but the moment wouldn't allow it. My mom, sitting next to Grandpa, with an equally vacant stare, was the second youngest of the family of twelve. Her thoughts could have been anywhere. Of course, like the others, she was trying to deal with the absence of her brother. Perhaps she was already anticipating her next loss since Dale had told her he wouldn't make it back from his next tour. His anger was too deep to reason and too painful to suppress. It's also possible she was thinking of the thirteenth person in the picture.

One row in front of Dale, to the right of Grandpa, deep in the belly of my mother, was me. When Mom told me I was there, I don't think she intended, nor could have imaged, the impact that fact would have on me.

To know that I was, to some small degree, present during such a difficult trial made me keenly aware of and fascinated by my family's history. I never had the privilege of meeting Dale or Sammie. I've heard countless stories and know that the brothers were outrageous, loud, bold, and the closest of friends. I also know, from within the womb, I responded to both of their voices, kicking and twisting which, in my mind, means we had some type of significant relationship.

A few weeks after the family portrait was taken, Dale was killed in Vietnam. His plan had come to fruition as he went down in a blaze of glory, anger, and unimaginable sorrow. He died a hero but I won't go into the details because all that matters when a loved one dies is dealing with the pain of their absence. Thirty-seven years later each family member still deals with that pain on a daily basis.

LIFE OF PRIVILEGE

Growing up in a trailer park(s) tends to alter one's perception of wealth. Unbeknownst to me, my mother and I were poor. This little secret was kept from me for many years as I enjoyed the same lifestyle as those kids who grew up in stationary houses. I had a Stretch Armstrong, a Spiderman with a retractable grappling hook, a bike mounted CB radio, and my own basketball goal nailed to a sycamore tree. In short, I had it all. The effects of low-income living were hidden from me by the fact that my mother worked so many jobs. Back before people were watching HGTV and doing-it-yourself was an empowering pastime for trendy homeowners, my mom was hanging wall paper in practically every newly constructed house in town. The extra cash paid for various cuts of beef, bags of potatoes, and whatever toy was currently holding the must-have status among Ozark's younger citizens. Paper hanging was the perfect fit for a single mother looking for a second job. Mom couldn't afford a babysitter, so I would tag along and play in the empty houses while she went about her work. Perhaps I didn't have her full attention, but at least there was someone there to tell me to be quiet, stop running, put that down, stay out of there, keep my shoes on, stop throwing rocks, and to make me wait until we get home to use the bathroom because those toilets have yet to be connected to the sewer line.

In the summer 1992 I worked as a camp counselor at an exclusive summer camp in Maine. At this point in my life I had graduated college and was halfway through a Master's degree. Connie, my future wife, and I had decided to get away from the university and just take it easy for the summer. This was my fourth summer working as a camp counselor, so I thought I was prepared for anything. Since this was a girl's camp, I would only be teaching archery for the summer – no real counseling needed. Connie, on the other hand, was assigned to supervise counselors – a buffer to handle differences between children and their cabin counselors.

When I was a boy, I attended basketball camp and church camp. The biggest differences between those camps were the presence of a Bible at one and no girls at the other. Neither had air conditioning and both had ticks, chiggers, and mosquitoes. The activities at church camp included singing praise, craft time, snack time, and one daily group activity that was meant to serve as a social mixer. The only real chance a boy might have to meet a cute girl at church camp was during dodge ball. I was spot on with my aim, so I could get the attention of any girl I wanted, but they usually didn't warm up to being smacked in the face with a red rubber ball. Still, I would smile and wave as they got back up, hoping they'd remember me later. Basketball camp activities included basketball.

The summer camp in Maine was what one might refer to as the other side of the tracks, although it was actually on the other side of the country, which was figuratively on the other side of the world. Activities for the Maine camp included, rock climbing, canoeing, sailing, photography, ballet, acting, musical theatre, swimming, archery, tennis, basketball and hiking. They even had camp within a camp as there were many day trips, as well as overnight trips, that included mountain climbing and whale watching. That's right, whale watching. Once, when I was at church camp, I got to see a squirrel wrestle a raccoon for a ham sandwich near the Bear Creek snack shop. Never saw a whale, though. Still haven't.

If you were lucky enough to be a girl attending the Maine Summer Camp for really, seriously wealthy children, there was a staff of hundreds whose sole purpose was to ensure that you got your $15,000 to $25,000 (depending on which package your parents chose) worth of fantastic summer memories. The main house of the Maine camp was a one hundred year old beautifully built and meticulously preserved building that was as rich in history as it was in market value. The walls were adorned with old photos of girls wearing the dress of their day, enjoying exciting activities like posing or sitting.

The wood floors creaked in a nostalgic way, reminding you that even the tongue-in-groove planks had history. Large screens circled the entire building to allow the optimum breeze to keep each room at the optimum temperature. The lawn, and I'm talking many acres of rolling, perfect for strolling, hillside was meticulously manicured to two and one quarter inches. While nice little animals like birds and chipmunks were allowed, there were no pesky pests like rats, mosquitoes or any buzzing, biting annoyances. I used to think that this little slice of heaven was so nice that the devil's creatures knew better than to enter. However, one night, around 2:00 in the morning, I noticed a chemical truck driving slowly through the property as it sprayed every tree, bush, and shrub with a concoction guaranteed to keep anything with a pincher, stinger, teeth or claws far from paradise.

Connie and I arrived a week early to help prepare the camp for the arrival of America's best and brightest female minds. We moved beds from storage barns to the cabins, anchored the docks just off the lake's shore, cleaned, polished, and shined every aspect of an already beautiful environment. It's hard to exaggerate the serenity of such an amazing place. I kept thinking that if I sat in the Adirondack lawn chair and stared at the main house long enough, that the young Katherine Hepburn would emerge from within, take a deep breath and proclaim the day as, "Marvelous!" Of course, this tranquility, this peacefulness was all experienced before the girls arrived.

With camp completely prepped, the counselors all gathered at the main house on yet another gorgeous morning. It was close to noon and we had been waiting for over an hour when I heard a low rumble. It sounded like distant thunder but the sky was as clear as a whistle. The rumble grew stronger and began to take on a rhythm. "What is that?" We all looked around as the sound grew stronger and seemed to surround us. As I turned toward the only road leading into camp, the rumble became a chant, hundreds of prepubescent voices strong. "Thunder! Thunderation! We're the best camp in the nation!" Louder and stronger. Louder and stronger. "Thunder! Thunderation! We're the best camp in the nation!" A line of at least eight luxury tour buses rocked as they rolled down the road directly toward us, dust billowing from under their heavy-duty frames. "Thunder! Thunderation! We're the best camp in the nation!" The fear I felt must have been similar to what unarmed villagers experience when a modern and powerful army loaded with rocket launchers, grenades, throwing knives, land mines, hairdryers and trust funds invades their hallowed sanctuary.

The ground vibrated as the counselors took a frightened step back. The camp director sensed our unease, "Steady. Steady!" For a brief moment, I considered going AWOL, which would mean hiking back to Arkansas. I was good in the outdoors but I knew that once I ventured beyond the chemical barrier protecting the camp, my ass would be eaten by savage mutant mosquitoes who had been dreaming of human flesh while being forced to settle for toxic-infected, lost squirrels blinded and weak from ingesting contaminated nuts. By the time I snapped back to attention, the buses were upon us and the doors burst open. A six-foot tall nine year old with a sinisterly smooth pony tail pointed in my direction, "You! Get my bags to Mustang Cabin, third bunk on the bottom. Now!"

"Yes, sir!" I blurted as I hoisted the four hundred pound patent leather duffle bag over my shoulder. Two vertebras in my lower back snapped and my spinal cord partially severed under the heavy load, but I knew better than to complain to a future C.E.O. whose lawyers were probably watching at that very moment via satellite. I prayed I wouldn't accidentally glance at her butt.

The smugness that I had arrived with a week earlier had dissipated. I wasn't going to be the cool, college guy that the kids really liked. No, indeed, I was a man-servant to children with an I.Q. that made my own look like a 10:30 a.m. ticket number from the line at a lunch deli, "Now serving number 17, number 17."

And so the routine of summer had begun. Wake, eat, teach archery, crack a joke, get confused and/or angry stares, eat, teach archery, crack a joke…it didn't take long for the Mondays, Tuesdays, Wednesday's, etc., to wear away leaving only days. The only way to know for certain that a new week had started was that we ate bagels for breakfast on Monday. After I had eaten lox and cream cheese for the seventh time, a strange buzz began moving through the camp, a type of giddiness was spreading fast. It started with the youngest campers and eventually pierced the stern exterior of the mid-teen veterans. Guests were on their way. But this wasn't just the locals or a visiting sister-camp of like-minded youths from across the lake, this was a once-a-summer special engagement – the parents were coming.

Of course, I was terrified. Being from Arkansas, I always traveled with an ingrained humility that made me think others, those from classier states in the union, would be appalled by my mere presence. But these weren't simply classy people, they were the elite who were born wealthy and raised wealthy. These people ate wealthy for breakfast and, when they grew tired, they slept on wealthy. I was a nervous wreck the night before the parents arrived. I dreamed that corncob pipes were growing out of my ears and that no matter how many times I tried to put on shoes, I would suddenly become barefooted when anyone looked at me.

I wish that this paragraph could be packed with funny, ridiculous examples of how terrible the parents were or how they treated me like a hillbilly. The truth is they were very polite and, at most, I was exposed to slight indifference. My biggest shock was watching my adolescent masters turn into doting children, clinging to their parent's leg, talking non-stop about the fun they had experienced while soaking up every crumb of attention the parents could toss their way.

At first I was rather cynical. I wondered what the little demons were after…a contraband cassette player was what I most often guessed. The only music allowed was taps in the morning and whatever tunes spilled out of dance class around three o'clock in the afternoon. Once again, I was wrong. The younglings were sincere. In fact, the following afternoon, when visiting weekend was over, the little ladies were devastated. The older girls had been there before and were trained in quick recovery techniques. They had an image to uphold, and tears are counterproductive to being cool. But the seven to ten year olds were a different story.

It's easy to judge brats when they do stupid things like sneak out of their cabin to dance naked on the main lawn while wrapped in glowing necklaces or accuse a counselor of sexual misconduct because they got caught stealing (I should clarify that I was NOT said counselor!), or when they casually cheat at a sport in an attempt to break the all-time record. But despair is the one tie that binds us all together. I won't go into detail about the behavior and emotional torment that most of the kids suffered while watching their parents drive away because it's really not all that funny. However, if you have ever felt any kind of heartbreak, you quickly understand that these spoiled little shits had probably just endured the type of scarring moment that they will one day retell for six months of Tuesdays at noon for $500 an hour.

I wanted to tell the girls that they shouldn't worry because in six short weeks they would be right back in mommy and daddy's arms. But that would have been a lie. Most of the kids weren't going back home. Most didn't arrive at camp from home. They came from, and would return to, boarding schools. A lot of the kids were seeing their parents, not just for the only time during the summer, but one of the few times they would see them all year.

You may be asking yourself how it's possible that these kids are raised like lottery winning orphans. Who's to blame? I don't know. You can't blame the parents. They probably went through the same cycle, so it seems completely normal to them. Besides, long before the parents began breeding, they were free to travel the world without a single concern.

Honestly, you can't expect them to take their kids with them if they suddenly decide to have dinner in Paris. You also wouldn't expect sensible parents to leave their loved ones with a babysitter if they should need to participate in Brazil's week long Carnival. The only logical solution is a boarding school. It's a win-win-win all the way around. The kids get hundreds of peers with identical problems wearing identical clothes and never having to deal with the pressure of what the folks will think. The parents never have to worry about being out late or worrying if they'll wake up the kids. The boarding school never has to worry about Tom Bodet muscling into the neighborhood and turning their three-hundred-bedroom, six-kitchen, forty-bath mansion into a Motel 6.

As the sun set on summer camp, Connie received the news that her beloved grandmother had died. She had raised Connie from a very young age. We sat on the shores of the lake in silence for many hours of many evenings as Connie tried to image what life would be like now. A week later, my grandmother passed away and we started the whole grieving process all over again.

With all the drama of family deaths and the end of camp rapidly approaching, I pulled out my phone card and gave mom a call. While she was attempting to console me by sharing comforting stories of my deceased grandmother, I felt a tap on my shoulder. I asked mom to hold on as I turned around.

"Dude, can you hurry up? I'm having a crappy day, and I seriously need to call my therapist." By the look of her fraying French braid and her untucked camp tee, I knew this nine-year-old had a more serious problem than I. "Thanks, Mom. Talk to you later. Gotta go."

TRAILER PARK BULLY

Every person living on the planet can tell you, without a nanosecond of hesitation, the name of his or her grade school bully. No matter what that bully's name was, everyone who was tortured by that asshole will pronounce the name with a certain amount of disgust and superiority as if to take one more shot at revenge.

If you think really hard, you can probably come up with several individuals that could qualify as a bully. Bobby Shears was a tough little scrapper who would go head to head with anyone in the third grade. He ruled the playgrounds with an iron fist and thrilled at the opportunity to rumble. He was a dirt-faced, shaggy-topped blonde who was bone-thin and as fidgety as a crack addict living on Splenda. Fortunately, Bobby's reign of terror ended in the fifth grade – coincidentally, this was the same year that Bobby stopped growing. He still cursed and caused trouble but everyone just brushed him aside like shopping mall fart odor. Don't cry for Bobby, I believe he went on to become a savvy businessman. I have a distinct memory of him standing in the corner of the playground trading a plastic bag for cash. Trading a plastic bag for cash!? Who would have thought that a bruiser would have such creative and entrepreneurial skills?

William Tale was the guy to watch out for in high school. He was every centimeter of 6'4" and many believed he was at least thirty-five years old. The only real run-in I ever had with him was my freshman year. I had recently broken my collar bone and was walking through the halls when William rushed by and slapped my books out of my one good arm. Had I not been disabled, I probably would have been afraid. However, the thought of William harassing an injured student made me see him for what he really was – a turd-for-brain that was too stupid to qualify as a Neanderthal. This assessment was confirmed a few months later during lunch. William had just watched me break apart crackers to add to my vegetable soup. He scoffed, swiped up a handful of his own crackers and proclaimed that, "Real men do it with one hand." With that, he used his awe-inspiring, vise-grip-of-death, bone-crushing right hand to completely crush four whole crackers with one hand. I'm not kidding. I saw it. He completely pulverized those crackers as if they were something much more fragile than crackers. As horrified as I was by his awesome and terrible strength, I took comfort knowing that I could probably break at least three crackers and that manhood was well within sight.

Despite the grand efforts of Bobby Shears and William Tale, the bully of my childhood can be no other than Reginald "Reggie" L.F. Towers. And, like most of my recollections, this one begins in a mobile home.

Mom and I lived in the McNutt trailer park at the time. I should mention that this wasn't our personal trailer park, it was owned by my uncle so all profits realized rightfully went to him. Reggie lived across the street from the park in a home without tires…poor bastard – they were stuck there. From what I remember, Reggie was from a stable family. He had a mother, a father, and a sister. Even though Reggie was a bully, he and I played together, and I would often hang out at his house, a tarpaper covered two-bedroom transitional. Granted, a house without siding isn't very attractive, but the fact that it was always under construction did have a few advantages, the biggest being that scrap material was always available for front yard bonfires.

Reggie's family was very different from mom and I. C.T., Reggie's dad, was one of the most insanely intense men I've ever known. Imagine a washed-out, shell-shocked surfer just returning from a tour in Nam, with shaggy, mustard colored hair, balding about eight inches above his protruding, tentacle-like eyebrows, having thrown back five double-shots of espresso and thinking he just heard a pin being pulled from a hand grenade while being stung in the ass by a bumble bee. That was C.T. twenty-four/seven. Simply saying "Howdy" to C.T. was as nerve wrecking as playing Russian roulette with Christopher Walken – and I mean the real Christopher Walken, not just his character in The Deer Hunter. I don't remember whether or not Reggie's mother was a good cook, but I know she loved the convenience of butter sticks. Sue Joe Ann, Reggie's kid sister, was always being fed sticks of butter as if they were candy bars. I can't knock butter as a stand-alone treat because I've never tried it. Butter may indeed be delicious, but it does have one side effect - I distinctly remember Sue Joe Ann constantly shitting herself. The trailer park kids would be playing when, all of sudden, Sue Joe Ann would squat down, get all red faced, then slowly stand and shuffle home with an obvious ode de feces wafting in all directions. Some might think it odd for a five year old to unload whenever the mood hits, maybe it was a cry for help or a sign of unrest in the home. To the contrary, I always found the Towers to be rather tight knit.

I have a distinct memory of spending a day with the Tower's at the edge of the mighty Arkansas River. Mom was busy that day, so I suppose the Tower's were technically baby-sitting me. Most baby sitters would be too uptight to allow a six-year-old the pleasure of swimming in the Arkansas River. Not the Towers. They either had a great deal of trust in my scissor kick or didn't think that the little ol' quarter-mile-wide river had the strength to wash me away. As fun as that fight for survival was, the most perplexing part of the day came at dinner time. We were sitting around the plywood table when I commented how delicious the meat was. C.T., gnawing on sinewy bone, proclaimed, "Horse is good." Surely, he was joking. Right? Probably.

Since I didn't have a father around, I was always fascinated by C.T. and Reggie's relationship. One summer evening, Reggie and I were walking directly in front of the white church at the edge of the trailer park when we heard a gun shot, a rather distinct and unsettling sound, even in Arkansas. Another shot rang out as dirt scattered near our feet. Just as we were about to panic, we realized that we weren't under attack at all, it was just C.T. playing a joke on us. It was like a heightened version of peek-a-boo.

In addition to Guess-Who's-Shooting-At-You, C.T. and Reggie also wrestled. While bouncing up to the Tower's front door one Saturday morning, the father and son were playing smack down on the couch. The front door was open, so, as I approached, I had the equivalent of a ring side seat. Since Reggie was big for his age, he was able to give the old man a run for his money. But, in a few moments, C.T. pinned his son. I had seen pro wrestling on TV and knew that steel chairs and ladders were fair game, so I wasn't necessarily shocked to see a leather belt used as a sparring tool. Reggie tried to gain an advantage by pretending to be hurt but ol' C.T. didn't fall for it. Finally, Reggie played possum, but I didn't stick around to see how that strategy worked out.

For some reason or another, Reggie's behavior started getting aggressive and a might unpredictable. I decided to omit the details of the event that first made me realize Reggie might be someone I should be weary off. The event illustrates Reggie's love of animals, a certain black lab to be exact. Now, I know what you're thinking and shame on you. Sometimes things aren't as disturbing as you might imagine. For example, would you have ever guessed that the lab was on top? Didn't think so.

I don't have an accurate memory of when Reggie and I went from buddies to a more predator/prey type of relationship. Regardless, running home everyday from school became quite common as Reggie was always looking for someone with whom he could play a quick game of Punch-the-Head. What God didn't bless me with in good looks, he more than made up for with endurance. The three o'clock bell signaled the end of school for most kids, for me, it was like a starter's pistol. I took plenty of bruises on the playground, but the teachers always interrupted the assaults. After school encounters were a matter of survival because there were no teachers there to break up the skirmish. I needed every second's worth of a head start I could get.

The biggest problem with running from Reggie every day was that I was, in essence, serving as his personal trainer. The more we ran, the faster he became and the more endurance he gained. A safe lead was a thing of the past, and I knew my days were numbered.

3:08 p.m., Thursday, I made it all the way down Gibson Street and had turned left onto Alston Street. Normally, Reggie had given up his pursuit by now. Not today. He was in great form as we made a right on Carver Drive. Our footsteps were slightly off beat since I was so much smaller and had a shorter stride. We ran with an impossible rhythm, like trying to dance to the Back Street Boys with Kenny Chesney wailing a ballad in your other ear. It was the kind of awkward, distracting noise that makes breathing under duress all the more challenging. The trailer park was finally in sight, which would usually provide comfort on a normal day. A half block later, and I was getting desperate. To my shock, Reggie picked up the pace as we blew past his house. "I'm going to die!" was all I could think. "I'm going to die!" "I'm going to die!" "I'm going to die!" "I'm going to die!" "I'm going to die!" "Voy a morir!" I was so scared I spoke Spanish for the first time, probably a by-product of seeing too many Clint Eastwood Westerns.

Exhaustion made my legs heavy, but what weighed down my spirit was the sudden laughter belting from Reggie as he knew I was in his clutches. I was still fifty yards away from home and running out gas with Reggie only a few paces back when I suddenly stopped and turned to face my tormentor. Oddly, he didn't slow down or even consider that

I might have some stupid plan to protect myself. He was so frighteningly confident that he actually picked up speed, perhaps angered that I had stopped his thrill of pursuing prey.

With four lanky strides between us, my knees buckled as I bent down and my eyes began to roll heavenward. Reggie's eyes widened as his claws extended and his mass leaned forward for the fatal pounce. With death swooping in, I pushed hard against the earth, throwing my arms as high as I could and stretching every joint in my body to its maximum length. For the first time in many tries, I was able to jump high enough to grab the t-bar of Mrs. Talson's clothesline just above my head. Both hands flexed tightly shut as I lifted my knees and then thrust my worn out sneakers directly into the smiling mug of Reggie Towers. Bam! Boom!

Bam! That was the sound of shoes striking a fast moving face. Boom! That was the thud of a thug suddenly reversing his direction and landing on his back. I hung like a monkey for a few seconds, swinging back and forth, the joy of victory quickly replaced by the dread of a possible homicide. Unfortunately, Reggie wasn't dead. By the time I dropped back to earth, he was sitting up, dazed and still pissed. I bolted. He gave chase.

One knock that people have against mobile homes is that they don't insulate against loud noises, a fact that saved my skinny ass on this day as Mom heard me screaming and came to the door to investigate. I leapt onto the porch and hid behind the one person I knew would never let anything happen to me. As she chastised the bully for picking on her son, I peeked around momma bear to laugh and sneer and wallow in my triumph over evil. I was a god – with a little "g."

That night, I dreamed I was the bionic man. It was the episode where Steve Austin does battle with Big Foot – freaking' awesome show! I leapt over a river in slow motion. When the sasquash threw a giant boulder at me, I pulverized it with my iron fist.   And finally, I beat down the big fella with a redwood tree that I jerked out of the ground. Of course, I didn't want to hurt B.F, but he had made me mad. It was a fearsome battle but, in the end, I was the only one standing. The monkey on my back had been tossed to the ground and stomped into submission. It was a beautiful dream.

The next day at school, I was retelling my real-life conquest of Reggie to two of my friends. We walked down the sidewalk toward the playground; a starry-eyed friend on each side, each one slack-jawed at my courage and Spiderman-like abilities. About the time I said, "…right on his ass!" we walked around the corner, and I found myself face-to-face with Reggie and his two sidekicks. An already unfair fight of three on three was reduced to three and me before I even knew my posse was gone. Quicker than I could beg for mercy or eke out a girly scream, Reggie's buddies had pulled my arms behind my back, and my short lived triumph abruptly came to an end with several blows to the gut. I fell to the ground amidst laughter and, without a word being said, a message had been sent and received.

That officially ended the possibility of Reggie and I scheduling any future play dates. I ceased bragging about my kung-fu kick and, rather surprisingly, Reggie ceased chasing me home. All and all, it was a pretty good trade.

Months later, Reggie was shipped off to some type of disciplinary school for kids who show promise as assassins or C.E.O's. The last time I saw C.T., Reggie's dad, was my sophomore year in high school. He was in the bank where mom worked, and I was in the back room cleaning, emptying trash cans, etc., for some extra pocket money. C.T. saw me and shuffled back to tell me how I was too timid of a rebounder. He came to most of the basketball games and wanted to give me a few pointers. C.T. pointed up in the air to an imaginary basketball hoop, took an aggressive box-out position with his knees bent, elbows out, and began bumping me around the room. The aroma of urine and alcohol was distracting, but I tried my best to pay attention. I have to admit, C.T. must have been a hell of rebounder because, try as I might, I couldn't get around that crazy nutter to get out of the room. If you've never been trapped in a small room with a physically belligerent mad man, it's about as intense as riding a tricked-out, cheap-ass, carnival Ferris wheel with a wolverine locked in your spinning steel cage.

Not long after my private basketball lesson, C.T. chose the express checkout and fired a shotgun slug into his head. I don't know what happened to Reggie, but I really believe that C.T.'s decision to send him away was done out of concern rather than frustration. Reggie's mom and sister fell completely off the radar. I've never heard a word about them but I do know it's possible for a mother and child to make a go of it alone. I like to think they saved enough money to get a real nice mobile home and lived happily ever after with no bad guys or bullies. I kept their wish simple to increase the odds of a happy ending.

ELECTRIC CRACKER

I've always admired people who were naturally, instinctively, effortlessly cool. Paul Newman from "Cool Hand Luke" was a bit of a stubborn ass, but man was he cool. Have you ever cheered so hard for a chronic loser? Any early Clint Eastwood Western can teach you all you need to know about the art of cool. Hell, half the time Mr. Eastwood doesn't even have any lines. He just stands there with that badass, ice-cold stare and you can't look away because he's so freakin' intriguing. There's never been a performance that scored as high in pure coolness as Eastwood's "The Outlaw Josey Wales." Of course, you can't have a conversation about cool without mentioning the godfather of cool. (Don't even talk to me about James Dean! Yes, he's cool, but no way does he make the holy trinity of cool. No way.) The only other man who must be on this list is Jack. I'm not even going to mention his last name because if you don't know about whom I'm talking, then you aren't socially equipped to understand this topic. Who else could play a role with a bandage across the bridge of their nose for an entire movie and create an all-time classic cool performance? Who else could play an elderly, hypochondriac who gets the young chick to fall for him and we believe it? Who else could utter the line, "You make me want to be a better man." and remain masculine? Jack – there's no one else.

Narrowing the list of the all-time coolest people to three is pretty easy. Honestly, this list would probably be the same if produced by any other astute historical researcher. But what if this list were expanded to four? Aahh…now things get pretty damn interesting. (Stop with the James Dean! I totally dig him but he's a seven slot at best.) First of all, the further down the list you go, the tighter the standards must be. You have to have some type of system to compare the talents of Brando, Pacino, DeNiro, etc. Most historians would suggest that a body of work or a minimum period of impact be established to weed out one hit wonders. Still, I believe an impact is an impact. Look at humans and asteroids. One has an impact duration of about one quarter of a second and the other has been around for thousands of years – but both would be viable nominees for Most Likely to Destroy the Planet. And with that, I nominate, for the fourth coolest person to ever live – Electric Cracker.

Electric Cracker didn't burst onto the scene until my sophomore year, but his story began a year earlier. The 80's have often been referred to as the Decade of Decadence. Bright colors, flashy clothes, and that super clean preppy look had permeated all aspects of culture. Not a single movie shot in the 1980's could be mistaken as having been filmed in any other decade, despite genre or period. No one escaped the look or the cheesy attitude. But a select few extraordinary individuals were able to transcend cultural phenomenon to make a lasting impression. Electric Cracker was a normal enough guy until late one summer evening in 1984. He and a buddy were hanging out at a cheerleader's house who happened to had a rare talent. Rumor had it that she could service two people at once and, although the experience would certainly be awkward, what's the big deal if no one gets hurt? Electric Cracker, feeling frisky, decided to go for it almost as a joke because getting a perm, at that time, wasn't all too common for guys. But from the time that plastic shower-cap looking thing was removed, after twenty minutes to allow the chemicals to retrain the hair with the perfect amount of curl, it was obvious to all that a star had been born. Even E.C., as he would later come to be known, could only stare at his glamorous image in the mirror. It was truly electrifying.

Understandably, the ladies immediately responded to the new look. But something else began to happen. It was almost as if he had been bitten by a radioactive spider or was wearing a magical amulet. His powers began to grow.

The sudden increase in vertical jump and the late burst of speed on the track were only a few of the tangible observations that caused heads to turn. Perhaps it was the confidence of knowing that his new, wavy hair was less likely to shift during intense workouts. Maybe it was a self-perpetuating process of adulation feeding esteem and thereby tapping into those little known, and less understood, powers and prowesses that only a few humans are able to maximize. Regardless, Electric Cracker was changing.

E.C. had a completely normal name until his sophomore year. Nearly twelve months after the notorious Second Street perm, he experienced a life changing moment that effectively killed the old him. A friend, returning from a visit to a cousin in Fort Smith's North side, had been to see an amazing new movie that was taking America's youth by storm. A powerful film of daring and defiance was inspiring all who witnessed it and a wave a cultural change was quickly swelling. It was the type of movement in which Electric Cracker longed to participate.

"Breakin'" wasn't too far removed from "Easy Rider." This new break dancing movie was a subculture flick that affected people across the boundaries of social standing. E.C. had only heard of the movie and was already a student of this new movement. His friend came bearing more than just the retelling of a cinematic experience. He also brought, and revealed, the secrets of one of the most mind-boggling mysteries of the twentieth century. Only the Shroud of Turin and the Rosetta Stone have garnered more thought provoking research than Michael Jackson's moonwalk. Was it supernatural? Did Mr. Jackson sell his soul to the devil for the gift of floating backward above the ground? What sort of witchcraft allowed this man to defy the laws of gravity?

The code had been cracked. As E.C.'s buddy moonwalked across the linoleum kitchen floor, E.C. took in every nuance of the magical footwork. Within seconds, E.C. had perfected the movement and was hungry for more. It only took a week for E.C. to locate a rare book containing illustrations and actual photos of break dancers in action. Now that E.C. was in the know, he had a responsibility to protect these ancient secrets and keep the book under lock and key.

As any committed artist will tell you, the road to fulfillment, perfection, enlightenment, etc., etc., is all uphill and never ending. And so it was with Electric Cracker. His book of break-dancing had been tossed aside like a crack addict's pack of cigarettes. Bandana...check. Parachute pants...check. Fingerless gloves...check. He had it all but needed more.

Racism aside, it was a fact that the black community knew more about the inner-workings of break dancing than the white man. Much like voodoo, there were certain instinctual nuances that came natural to blacks. A white man would need guidance to master those same skills. Sadly, there were only a few black families in Ozark and only one of those families had kids. Those kids were raised among white children and had been forced to repress most of their cultural impulses just to blend in. Electric Cracker needed a mentor, a true unadulterated master to point him in the direction of musical, rhythmic expression beyond the limits of modern dance. Electric Cracker was getting desperate.

About twenty miles North of Ozark was a facility called Cass Job Corp. Think of a womanless community for wayward teens, young men, and some older men who just couldn't get their shit together. It was similar to a halfway house...something somewhere halfway between a prison and a job training center that boiled down to cheap labor to repair roads, bridges and what not. Periodically, a Job Corp bus would pull into town and allow some of the more behaved fellows to hang out for a few hours, take in some culture or a get a tasty cheeseburger. It had long been known that the Cass boys were excellent basketball players but, E.C. had heard that something else was going on way out in the Ozark foothills.

By the time Electric Cracker pulled onto the gravel driveway, darkness had fallen across the tiny valley and its institutional community that was built less than a hundred yards from a picturesque mountain stream. If not for the perpetual prospect of being assaulted, this would surely be a great place to live. E.C. cautiously stepped out of his truck and was instantly tipped off to where the action was by the deep thump of a boom box.

Stepping inside the enormous roll-up loading door to the aluminum, barn-inspired gym, E.C.'s eyes widened as he experienced a sensation that must be similar to what departed souls must feel when they open their spiritual eyes and find themselves standing in front of Heaven's pearly gates.

On one end of the court was an intensely competitive basketball game with highly skilled athletes playing with equal parts passion and playfulness. On the other end of the court was a large piece of cardboard with breakers taking turns showcasing their skills to the powerful downbeat of music so captivating that E.C. couldn't keep from doing the wave.

He paused for a moment wondering if perhaps he had been struck head-on by a semi while rounding one of the dangerous sharp cutback turns on his way through the mountains. Could he actually be standing in heaven at this moment?

"What up, cracker?" E.C. snapped out of his daze to see one of the young men apparently offering his assistance. Not only were these people unexpectedly polite, they somehow knew E.C.'s name.

"I need to know everything about break-dancing."

It was one of those life-changing nights that can change your life. By gaining such insight into a mysterious art, E.C. was suddenly at the forefront of a movement and a respected member of an extraordinary brotherhood. He eagerly observed every movement and took in all the advice he could before the supervisor turned off the lights and warned everyone to get to their bunks before punishments were dolled out.

"See ya later, Cracker!" E.C. nodded his appreciation and headed home newly skilled and forever changed.

In a town with nothing to do, the high school Home Coming dance was about as close to Mardi Gras as Ozark would ever get. The planning committee was formed within the first week of school and dating arrangements soon followed. The purpose of a Home Coming event is to welcome back students of the past, although none of them are allowed to attend the dance due to restrictions on interacting with minors and violations of the legal drinking age. However, every dance ever thrown at Ozark High featured at least one awkward moment where students would discover a couple of glassy-eyed, Wrangler clad, belt-buckled, moose-knuckled, thirty-something year old guys pitching their perfectly conceived plan that they were simply new transfers with a glandular problem. In short, the homecoming dance was always a culturally diverse collection of merry-makers.

Electric Cracker arrived an hour after the cafeteria/dance floor opened. He mingled, he shook hands, but mostly, he waited. Patience is essential to those with progressive or alternative ambitions in Northwest Arkansas, especially considering that the number of quality songs one can break to is extremely limited. The rap group Houdini was popular and would probably get some play but the Sugar Hill Gang would suffice in a pinch.

Since breaking is a largely territorial behavior and parallels the gangster's life, E.C. scanned the crowd to see if there were any rivals present. There were a few freshmen who played around with breakin' but they could barely do more than a basic wave with a little remedial robot – not enough to be considered an artist, nor a threat.

Immediately following Joan Jett's *I Love Rock N' Roll*, the D.J. rocked the party with one of the all-time greatest compositional pieces known to man -   Herbie Hancock's

Rockit. E.C. instinctively reacted to the hypotonic, powerful beat. He had been slightly nervous to show this new side to his peers, but, with a song so dynamic and alluring, E.C. found himself being swept away. He was actually standing inside the music.

He took to the floor with a slightly altered, although familiar, moonwalk as to not shock or frighten the crowd. After a triple heel spin, he crisply snapped into a futuristic version of the robot with subtle influences and the smooth transitions commonly seen in advanced versions of the wave. E. C. ignored the cheers and remained intensely focused on the music; listening, interpreting, reacting. He was a hip-hop puppet popping and breaking to the carnal, yet evolutionary, life-pulse of a sound created by one of music's most innovative innovators. It was this night that the legend of Electric Cracker was put into play.

It was only a matter of weeks until E.C. had formed a crew. Like Jesse James, Robin Hood, Puff Daddy, and Waylon Jennings, E.C.'s mojo grew by having a stable base of like-minded artists around him. Although groupies took longer to form than anticipated, word of the group's mad skills spread quickly and an opportunity for mass exposure was soon upon them.

About six miles East of Ozark is the sleepier little town of Altus. At the time, Altus consisted of eight beer joints, three wineries, two gas stations and a Catholic church. (These days, you can find a couple of great restaurants and some quaint antique shopping. Check out Fox's *A Simple Life*, Season One for more information.) Despite having a population of about six hundred, Altus has one weekend each year when the town becomes a tourist hot-spot known as Octoberfest! Or Wine Festival! Maybe it's the Wine-for-sell-fest! Anyway, it's big. So big, in fact, that it was critical to have popular entertainment for the masses.

E.C. and his posse were invited to perform which all but insured that they were about to burst into the regional spotlight as media coverage could easily spread as far as thirty miles. Channel 5, the only credible local news source, would be present and their cameras would be rolling. To prepare for such a big event, E.C. and the boys began training at the courthouse on Friday nights. All it took was an 8'x'8' piece of cardboard and a boom box to transform any location into a break-dancing wonderland. Press play, let the cassette roll, release the bass, and a crowd was sure to gather and gawk at the mystifying movements of these young innovators. Hordes as large as ten people weren't uncommon. Citizens were often so appreciative and encouraging that they would leave modest sums of money to help fund the cause. Electric Cracker was gaining excellent momentum with the festival only a few days away.

With matching camouflaged outfits already purchased, E.C sensed it was time to begin a more aggressive training routine. This eventually led him to take his graceful and fluid presentation to the floor with a backspin, a knee spin, and a nearly perfected version of the wrist spin. At last, he was ready for his regional premiere.

E.C. arrived a few hours early to scout the area, check sight lines, and confirm the levelness of the dance area. A Country band was warming up and one more would take the stage before Cracker time. It was only 11:00 a.m. but the wine was already flowing, as were the turkey legs and funnel cakes coated in glorious amounts of powdered sugar. Families took their time roaming from booth to booth partaking in, and taking home, the latest in arts and crafts. Kids sat perfectly still for face paintings but went crazy for the ring toss. A long line proved that the greased pig contest would once again be successful. In short, it was the perfect venue for a break-dancing exposition.

As always, a crowd gathered as the air began to thump with a beat that could only be generated by the primordial impulses of rap. E.C.'s boys took to the floor first as four robot-like figures wowed the spectators with mechanical movements and stop-motion dance moves. Finally, Electric Cracker slid onto the stage and immediately tapped into the familiar as he mime-danced the biggest and best moments from all three major sports by throwing a touchdown pass to himself, shooting a three-point basket, and hitting a monstrous home run. The show was flawless.

The crowd electrified. The only hitch came during E.C.'s finale. The worm was always a crowd pleaser but caused excruciating pain to the testicular area. E.C., for the love of his fans, did the worm forward and backward in one of the bravest performances since an injured Willis Reed hobbled into Madison Square Garden to rally the New York Knicks to victory. Look it up. It was brave. The crowd was so grateful for the performance that they clapped. Electric Cracker was even asked to give an autograph. Surely, it wouldn't be long before MTV or Puma would come knocking.

Somewhere in the Bible, there's a line something like, "When I became a man I put the foolishness of youth behind me." As Electric Cracker's reputation as a breaker grew, basketball, his first love, suddenly became less and less of a priority. He had found his calling and knew that all other pursuits were simply silly distractions. It wasn't long until trusted friends were replaced by new acquaintances. E.C., blinded by a dream, wasn't aware of his compromise in companions...but one old friend wasn't so willing to go away quietly.

East Side Park was the outdoor court with chain nets and an asphalt surface where Electric Cracker and his friend spent countless hours playing ball practically everyday, despite the temperature, time of day, rain or snow. It was a holy place for the two young men, not to be taken for granted and never to be disrespected. This b-ball tandem was known far and wide to dominate and defend this particular court as if each game were the last stand of some ancient battle. Players often came from other cities to challenge the duo and always left defeated.

But on one particular spring night, Electric Cracker crossed the line of friendship and turned his back on respect. Perhaps it was pride or the desperate need to reinvent himself that made E.C. choose East Side Park to practice his latest dance moves. As he and a couple of his crew members set up their cardboard training facility, E.C.'s best friend, who had been all but forgotten in the whirlwind of break-dancing fame, happened to show up at East Side with a few new friends of his own to play ball. It was as if each was cheating on the other and flaunting the fact that it didn't matter to either.

E.C. focused on his dance, but the old friend, let's say his name was Dominique, refused to let the night pass without incident. For a few days prior, Dominique had been spreading the rumor that E.C. was losing his skills as a "baller" and was disgracing himself by pursuing this break-dancing stuff. Of course, Dominique's accusations traveled quickly but E.C. had largely laughed off the insults, at least until this night.

It began with a few derogatory words shouted from the court to the cardboard in random spurts. E.C. tried to quiet the doubter by pushing dance beyond the limits of human experience, hoping to make his old pal a believer. To the contrary, it wasn't long before each insult was followed by a thunderous dunk that rattled and shook the steel backboard and echoed a challenge across the park. Electric Cracker was being called out.

"Let's go! Let's do it.!" E.C. wearing his favorite camo pants with a matching shirt and contrasting wrist bands, stomped toward the court ready to defend his hoop skills.

"What's the point? You haven't played in a month. It won't even be close."

"Give me the ball." Electric Cracker walked to the top of the key as the ball bounced his way. His fierce determination was slightly worrisome to Dominique who hadn't really expected his barbs to evolve into a man-to-man showdown.

"Check." E.C. flipped the ball to Dominique, who assumed a defensive position and tossed the ball back to E.C. Both sides had now officially acknowledged their readiness to engage. Electric juked left and bolted to the right. Dominique staggered and quickly recovered in time to see Electric reverse directions, spinning back to the left and banking an impossible left-handed scoop shot.

"Luck." quipped Dominique, but he knew better. He had seen this shot a thousand times and knew there would be more to follow as the battle continued. Electric Cracker, despite the lack of recent training, was on his game like never before. The wicked crossover, the out-of-reach fade away jumper, and the baby hook were all present and accounted for. Electric had a spring in his step that hadn't been felt for some time. The rhythm of the game suddenly consumed Electric as he played with a combination of joy and rage that is seldom obtained and rarely controlled. Dominique fought valiantly but was overwhelmed by a man on a mission to prove that he had not taken the wrong path.

As Electric Cracker's final shot fell threw the chain net to punctuate an indubitable victory, the break-dancer turned to walk back toward his boom box and realized that it was he who had been soundly defeated. Dominique had lost the contest but had proven his point: Cracker had traded his best friend for downbeat and a moonwalk. Cracker turned and walked away quickly, not as a sign of disrespect, but to hide his shame. For the first time, E.C. had an unadulterated view of what he had become.

As the late, great actor J.T. Walsh said in the movie *A Few Good Men*, "I am proud neither of what I have done, nor of what I am doing." I must now tell you that I am Electric Cracker. For years I've fought to hide that part of my life hoping it would fade away. But rule number one in a tell-all book is that you must tell all. Although I am not cured, I am a recovering break-dancer. Dominique, of course, is Wayne. He was the only friend who was brave enough to continue a buddyship beyond the embarrassment of performing a public backspin.

Soon after the incident at East Side, requests for me to bust a move were accompanied by a certain smirk. I suddenly felt like the slow kid who thought he did a great John Wayne impersonation, which actually sucked, but everyone asked him to do it because it was funny in a painful, sick kind of way. To this day I am haunted by the foolishness of my youth. The problem that recovering break-dancers encounter is that our peers seldom understand our level of regret. My wife, despite my constant pleading, will continue to tell her friends that I was a break dancer every time the subject of dance comes up. One friend stated a few years ago, "I was so sad that Gregory Hines died. He was such an amazing talent and brilliant dancer." My wife immediately responded with, "Jerry was a break dancer." Then, the inevitable request follows, "Really? Show me some moves." It is truly excruciating.

Now that I've completely come clean, can I finally breathe easy knowing that my secret is out? Can closure ever be obtained? No, absolutely not. Never. The reason my moonwalk will forever haunt me is because I believe, with concrete conviction, that somewhere in Northwest Arkansas, in some random attic, perhaps in the bottom of a box at a garage sale going on at this moment, is an old VHS bearing the label Electric Cracker, Altus Grape Festival 1985.

God help me.

BULLET HEAD

The one thing that separates youth from those who know better is their unflappable belief in invincibility. Being immortal, or believing you're immortal, is exactly what has allowed young people throughout history to accomplish things that were once thought impossible. Mozart, Louis XIV, and Michael Jackson all reached unfathomable heights at impossibly young ages. It's also the reason that young people lead the world in one bizarre statistic – Death Due to Stupidity. I have fond memories of my immortal days. Had I had the address to the Justice League, I would have certainly applied for Super Hero status. However, just like the Greek God, Icarus, I too tried to fly close to the sun only to get burned, figuratively speaking, of course.

Very few people perform stupid acts alone, which brings me to my friend, Darrell. I believe that we only make a few great friends in our lives. Sure, there are plenty of people that we like to hang out with, but the number that we truly click with, that we can finish their thoughts, or share a joke without saying a word, those people are too few and too damn far between. Darrell and I were new best friends from the instant we met. A few weeks later we hit the road and drove to West Texas to work at a summer camp during my freshman summer of college. When it was time to return to school, we decided to live in a house that Darrell's parents owned. It was a long drive to school, approximately thirty-five miles, but the house was on top of Petit Jean Mountain with a stunning view of the valley.

The problem with two immortals living together in such a remote area is that there's no adult, or authority figure, to say, "Hey, that's a really bad idea." Did I mention that there were a bunch of guns on the property? No? Well, as fate would have it, there were a bunch of guns on the property. And so, our story begins.

I can think of at least four incidents that could easily prove the point that Darrell and I should not have had guns around. Here's an example…One gun was a military issue, 38 pistol. It belonged to Darrell's dad, who lived in Georgia, and was retired from the military. I never thought it was a good idea to leave a loaded gun in the house, but Darrell had a different opinion. According to him, it was better to leave the guns loaded, that way, if a gun were ever needed, it would be ready. It's certainly not an illogical point of view.

At the time, I was going through my Western phase. *Young Guns* had recently been released, and I was doing all kinds of research on famous cowboys and outlaws. So, it only made sense that I needed to practice spinning a pistol on my finger. One Friday night, I had arrived to find the pistol, sitting in the closet, loaded. "Dude, why do you keep this thing loaded?" I removed the bullets and spent the next few minutes spinning the gun forward and backward, dropping it in the holster at the end of each set. At the end of the workout, I placed the gun back in the closet and went to scrounge up something for dinner.

Early the next morning, Darrell and I were planning to go for a hike. I was already dressed and ready to go but he was still in the shower. To avoid boredom, which is kryptonite to immortals, I decided to get in a few more minutes of gun trickery. I had just unloaded the gun the night before so checking for bullets would simply be a waste of time. I was really in a groove this particular morning, coming right out of a spin into a dead-eye aim. My quick draw was approaching lighting status.

I was beginning to think that Darrell had drowned when he finally emerged from the shower wearing only a towel. My patience was wearing thin, "Are you going hiking or not?" Darrell, and everyone who knows me, is well aware of my scheduling demands. If we're supposed to leave in ten minutes, be ready in ten-minutes, otherwise say you need twenty minutes! It doesn't matter that it's a weekend, that we have plenty of time, just hurry up. Darrell laughed at my impatience, and was about to say something that probably would have been very funny. Before he could get out his would-be-one-liner, I zipped the gun into a backspin and slammed it into the holster – BANG!

My heart not only stopped, it hid behind my vertebra for protection. Just like a Saturday morning cartoon, the bullet ricocheted off the floor, off the walls, and around the room for what seemed like thirty seconds. Darrell and I stared at each other, waiting for the other's head to explode the whole time that damn bullet was zinging around the room. At last, there was silence. Darrell patted himself down for bullet holes as I was racking my brains trying to remember how to breathe. With a sheepish head nod, Darrell agreed that it was probably a good idea to not the keep loaded guns in the house. That incident, however, is only a warm up to the reason I was forced to turn in my immortality card.

It was the end of the fall semester with only final's week remaining. Darrell and I were tired of studying and decided to grab a couple of guns and go for a walk. As we approached a rocky outcrop of cliff tops, Darrell veered to the right, but I wanted to walk out to the edge to see if there were any critters hanging out at the base of the cliff. Nothing. Darrell had continued on so I decided to take a shortcut to catch up. The cliff was approximately three stories high. To get an idea of where I was, place your hand flat on a table. Imagine me standing on the end of your middle finger with Darrell on end of your pointer finger. I decided to jump from one cliff to the next to make up some time. It was only about six feet so it wasn't exactly a challenge. I should mention that I had two guns with me. One was a 1920's model .22 rifle that my grandfather gave me. The other was a .22 pistol that my dad had given me. The pistol also had a hand-made holster that didn't have any type of strap to keep the gun from flying out. To make sure I didn't drop either gun, I held one in each hand and, yes, both were loaded.

I leapt across the chasm without a single doubt that I could make the distance. As a matter of fact, jumps like this were routine on hikes, nothing out of the ordinary. But there was one thing that was out of the ordinary. The last couple of days had seen freezing temperatures. What I could not see when I left the safety of the rock I was standing on, was the patch of clear ice that covered the rock I was currently flying toward. My foot shot forward, sending my center of gravity back toward the edge of the cliff, my balance was completely gone with no hope of recovery – I was falling. I stretched back toward the cliff I was previously standing on. The gap was six feet and I'm six feet two inches tall. My feet were still on the icy rock as my hands, still holding a gun apiece, slammed onto the opposing cliff. The good news is that my head didn't hit the rock, that bad news is that it hit the barrel of the rifle in my left hand. The worse news is…BANG!

The rifle discharged upon impact. The bullet didn't hit my head, rather it hit the rock wall one inch from my head and shattered, sending the bullet and rock fragments across my neck and forehead. I was dead. I knew it. I had to be dead. Well, I was at least deaf, but I knew death was coming. I couldn't hear it, but I could feel its icy grip take my balls and begin squeezing the life out of me. For a moment, I was too afraid to open my eyes. I honestly didn't want the last thing I saw to be the earth racing toward me as I fell from the cliff.

As the echo of the gun blast faded away, I heard my heart beating and assumed I might still have a chance. I opened my eyes to see a waterfall of blood trickling from my face to the ground below. Slowly, cautiously, I made my way to the spot I should have never left in the first place. Darrell hadn't moved. It appeared as if he, through sheer terror, had lost more blood than I had. His eyes were bulging out of his head, unable to conceptualize what was standing before him. I looked like act three Mel Gibson from any Mel Gibson movie. My face was completely covered in blood. Two wounds above my eyebrows caused a bloody stream to flow down between my eyes, running down each side of my face and onto my shirt. Neither of us said a word until, "I…ah… I think I should go to the emergency room." Darrell slowly nodded, "Yeah."

As we entered the emergency room, we were confronted with a long line. A nurse finally noticed me, and she approach to inquire about my condition. "I've been shot in the head, and I'd would like to see a doctor." I recommend that particular line to anyone in the emergency room, for it saves so much time.

About twenty minutes later, another nurse walked in with the x-ray and a bewildered look on her face, "You've got bullets all over your skull…" I was given a few shots to numb the various areas of impact and a doctor began digging around trying to find as many fragments as possible. The sound of metal scrapping on your skull is truly unforgettable. To his credit, the good doc was able to remove all but two pieces of lead. One annoying piece had lodged itself between my spinal cord and juggler vein and was too risky to retrieve. The other fragment was just under the rim of my right eye socket. It was close to the surface but the area contained delicate nerves that, if severed, could leave me with a droopy eye. I was already ugly enough and knew that a droopy eye, although very sexy on drunken women, wouldn't do me any favors.

Since the accident involved firearms, there was a brief investigation to rule out Darrell as a homicidal maniac. The next big concern was what lie we would both tell our friends. Although each wound was small, the swelling was intense. I looked like I had several small breasts implanted across the front of my head…and it wasn't as attractive as one might think. Like most stories, this one ends with my mom. I would be seeing her in two short days. To prepare her for the disturbing visual, I called and told her that I had fallen into a thicket of briars. Looking back at my lame attempt at a cover up, I'm sure mom instantly thought, "Oh my god, he's been shot."

It wasn't the fear of a near-death experience that made me turn in my rights to behaving like an immortal. I wasn't suddenly afraid to try crazy stunts. The real change was my ability to look into the future at the legacy that a stupid death leaves behind. My poor mom having to explain to the curious that her son died because he was jumping off a cliff with two guns in his hands was just too much to bear. Jumping on a hand-grenade, fine, no problem, there's certainly honor and bravery involved in that selfless act. I'm pretty sure I'll never accomplish anything great, nor will I have a profound impact on the world, but, as long I don't die doing something stupid that embarrasses everyone I know, then, perhaps my life will have not been a total loss. I can imagine nothing more humiliating than my life ending in an event that warrants my picture being on the cover of Time magazine. Going out with a bang is completely overrated, I know, I've stood at the edge and looked down upon the opportunity and can tell you that some marks simply aren't worth leaving.

THE GREAT DEBATE

A debate broke out among fellow college students early in my freshmen year. You have to be open minded, progressive in thought, and up-to-date on world events and current affairs. You must know when to improvise and when to stand your ground. Debates, whether they are formal or a simple happening near the Dean's private rose garden, are a battle ground for eager young minds to hone their intellectual and persuasive abilities. In short, great leaders are born while inferior players are cast aside.

On this particular autumn afternoon, we brash young Americans were heatedly discussing which of us had the coolest high school mascot. We agreed that the winner would be the candidate extolling the most wily, crafty, and cunning nature, while proving to be loyal and brave.

Kevin barged in with the eagles. "Blah, blah, blah... symbol of...blah, blah, blah bird of prey...blah." I sat back with a smugness of one who had already picked up on the ripe scent of victory. I would wait for the overconfident spewings of the collective unfortunate before I would make my move.

Next came the Cougars, the Lions, Bears, and Panthers. I suppressed a giggle. Come on, people! Cougars and Panthers are basically the same thing. Lions and Bears? Please. Why not just call yourselves the Football Team? It's just as imaginative and slightly more honest.

The next wave included offers of a more plausible ilk: Cowboys, Indians and Patriots. These were immediately and unanimously dismissed by the rest of the group because each was most likely stolen from a professional team and offered no applicable bearing upon the city it represented. A huge ruling in my favor! (I brazenly laughed but disguised my blunder by coughing – which then made me fart. I knew if I had been caught in a fart that all credibility would be lost. I casually inched my way over to the other side of the group and watched as offensive glances were thrown toward Kevin. Poor Kevin. I've never spoke of this mishap until now.)

Then came a curve ball. Thomas, whom I'd noticed was also sitting rather smugly, tossed in his Bearcats. This caused a moment of silence as the panel deliberated whether or not a hybrid was admissible. Since none of the aforementioned mascots actually participated in any sporting event, imaginary creatures were allowed entry. Damn! I'd have really gained a huge advantage with a reverse ruling.

Three mascots remained. Marcus entered the fray with his Badgers and we all knew the stakes had risen. We were all forced to admit that the badger is one of the fiercest creatures on the planet despite its diminutive stature. The little bastards stink to high heaven and are both fearless and territorial. But was it wily, crafty, or cunning? Marcus assured us that it was these things but Walker Anne (the oldest of the group, nearly 40, who was named after her Grandfather and his favorite Aunt) quickly countered with a correction. It was not the badger that was wily and cunning, no indeed that was the Wolverine! She sited an episode of Grizzly Adams where Flap Jack gets stuck in his own trap by a deadly and conniving wolverine. Although no one remembered the episode, we were all very familiar with Grizzly Adams and, being college students, were easily swayed toward environmental issues. A man living in the wild with a grizzly bear as his best friend added plenty of credibility.

After much discussion, the verdict was that even though the badger was a viable and respectable mascot, it did indeed lack the cunning and adaptability the committee was looking for. Walker Anne, although her mascot was a lame-ass Cardinal, had instantly become a force to be reckoned with. I sensed that my time had come.

There were only two candidates remaining before a final decision would be made. I didn't want to go last for fear I would give the appearance of superiority or arrogance. As I took a strong stance and used subtle body movements to capture the groups attention and signal my upcoming contribution, I visualized my mascot...rebellious, defiant, loyal, both reckless and purposeful. He was a survivor with no need for outside approval. He could brave any environment and would oppose any invader. He was...no, he is... (What's about to happen here is one of the first truly defining moments of my life. Sure there were literally hundreds of other events that shaped me and molded me into the person I am today, but it was this moment that I first experienced the "C" camera pull away. It's that moment when you suddenly see yourself in the actual situation you are currently in as if from a movie camera on a crane, almost as if your spirit is departing your body and you're looking back just before your empty shell collapses and you think, "That poor bastard has no idea what he's about to do." Yes, it was a moment like that. Whoosh! Just like that I was back in my body and before I could stop myself, I said...) "Hillbillies. I'm from Ozark, home of the Fighting Hillbillies."

I'm not talented enough to describe the next thirty seconds. But if I could give an accurate account, I would most likely use words like hilarity, pointing, confusion, shrinking, shrinking, awareness and humiliation. Those are good places to start. For the first time in my life, I realized I was a hillbilly. Suddenly, I mentally blocked out the external laughter with a shouting inner monologue of, "What the f#%k! Who in the hell came up with a fu*^ing hillbilly? Holy shit, I'm a stereotype! I'm from a town called Ozark in the state of Arkansas with an uckingfay hillbilly as mascot. What the f⊗ck!?" I suddenly pictured myself in the stands with my high school classmates chanting cheers like, "Who dat talking bout beatin dos Hillbillies? Who dat? Who dat?" Fuc💣✳ me! Can you imagine what the other teams were thinking? Why should they bother shouting insults at us when we're claiming to be hillbillies? It would be redundant! I finally make it to college to begin my march into adult life, doing my damndest to make an impact on the world, and I suddenly realize that I must do it as a hillbilly. Shit.

Oh, the mascot contest...? Kimberly O'Neal won with a Swampcat. I didn't stick around to find out what the hell it was supposed to be. It sounded pretty stupid though.

CRITTERS

Respect is one of the strangest concepts that we humans have ever invented. Over the years, respect has been applied to many different topics with an even larger number of meanings. Originally, we used respect as a system of rank. Youth were to respect their elders, yielding the right away to social issues and seeking the advice of those that had experienced more. But as generations passed by and times changed, we realized that most old coots had no idea what the hell they were talking about and their old fashion standards simply no longer applied.

Now that teenagers wear their underwear on the outside of their clothes and use their middle finger as a salutation, respect has been almost completely tossed out of the real world and seems to only thrive in the confines of sports interviews where lack thereof is a constant motivator for the underdog, which everyone claims to be.

Why exactly did respect get the shaft? When any concept has contradictory definitions, its survival can become exceptionally tricky. Growing up in a camouflaged county certainly skewered the essence of the word respect.

At the age of ten I was given my first hunting device. It was a single pump, spring-propelled B.B. gun. I'd love to brag about what a dead-eye shot I was, and, indeed, I was. All little boys have fantasies of living in the wild West and extolling justice with the aid of a lightening fast draw and laser accuracy. The simple truth about guns is that there is no other tool or implement on earth as easy to master. Any idiot with an attention span long enough to line up three points, two of which are fixed, will be deadly accurate. If you don't believe me, ask the good folks of Jonesborough, AR or any other city unfortunate enough to have been featured in Time Magazine for having trained their youth to play with guns.

But I had respect, so, I was different. At first, I only shot leaves in trees. It wasn't long before my steady aim could poke a hole in any leaf you cared to point out. In no time at all, I was sending B.B.'s through the stem of leaves to watch my target lazily float to the ground. Cans and bottles made the hit list as soon as I got myself to believe that these items were more biodegradable if they were in smaller, fragmented pieces.

Mastering one challenge is usually followed by a search for a greater challenge. That critical search is often where the common paths of all-people-created-equal diverge in the woods of social development. Some go to the left and chose to be leaders, doers, or innovators. Others will go right and follow base instincts, searching for something simple, easy, and immediate. I chose to leave all paths and sneak into the woods in hopes of killing a dangerous and menacing creature.

Birds are every B.B. gun owners first kill. Despite what you see on television, taking the life of another living being isn't an easy thing to do. Beyond the ethical struggle, there's the fact that most animals are quick, elusive, or winged. It starts with those little birds that you often see fluttering around in parking lots. They're mostly gray with a little bit of black on the throat and have a tiny, insignificant frame. Honestly, who would ever miss the presence of a bird like this? As members of the animal kingdom these guys barely outrank the worms they eat. Their real value is in the fact that they make excellent targets. Cardinals, Blue Jays, hummingbirds, and Red-winged black birds were in my sights many times, but I was never able to pull the trigger. The brighter the color, the more of a contribution I felt the animal was making to my own happiness. Crows on the other hand…seriously, who needs them?

At the age of twelve, I was given a .410 shotgun. It's a great gift for a little boy making the transition to being a man. By this age, a B.B. gun has diminutive value but a 12 gauge has too much kick. The .410 is the perfect tweener for rifle-philes and allows one to gain experience in both buckshot and slug mediums. Even in my middle teens, that gun was still a favorite companion in the forest. One day, Wayne and I were hiking with guns and we noticed something about thirty yards down the densely covered hillside. Since we couldn't tell what it was, we decided I should probably try to shoot it.

"Hmmm. What the hell is it…a beaver?" I postulated. Wayne shook his head as he kicked the fury beast over. "No, dumb-ass, look at the tail. I think it's a woodchuck. Nice shot though. Right through the head."

I remember, for a brief second, thinking, "Why did I shoot that thing?" But before I could come up with a good answer, we decided to continue up the hill to look for squirrels that had been terrorizing the villagers. Still, that damn question lingered like a mosquito bite on the balls; nagging but oddly entertaining.

Months later, still not having formulated an answer to the woodchuck riddle, (Not that one. I've never seriously wondered how much wood a woodchuck could chuck because if they can't, and they can't, then who the hell cares?) I found myself sitting at home with nothing to do. I tried to watch TV, but, there was a distracting amount of chirping going on in a tree at the edge of our driveway. The mulberry tree was packed with berries, and all the little birdies in the land were loading up like it was an all-you-can-eat buffet. I sat in the doorway in the back of the house with my old, trusty B.B. gun. Pump, aim, shoot, kill. It was kind of like mindless doodling. Pump, aim, shoot, kill. After a while, I ran out of B.B.'s but was too bored to go get any more. As I sat my gun down, I noticed something odd. It wasn't there before, but now it was at the forefront of my head like a fire truck's siren. It was silence. At first, I couldn't tell where it was coming from. The TV was still turned on, so it definitely wasn't coming from inside the house. I listened for a few more seconds and was convinced that the silence was coming from outside. I stood up and looked across the backyard. Nothing. Finally, I turned back to the driveway and was truly taken aback by the source of the overwhelming silence…it was the mulberry tree.

At the base of the tree was no less than twenty of the most silent birds you've ever heard and each one was screaming at me. There's a story of a boy who threw a rock at a bird and was heartbroken by his success. I found myself unable to look away from this updated, graphic remake. Suddenly, killing was no longer the innocent past time that it once was. Plus, I had a huge mess to clean up that Mom would totally lose her mind over if I didn't get it taken care of before she got home. I swore off killing and raced to the kitchen to get a trash bag and salad tongs.

Not long after the mulberry tree incident, I heard a hunter being interviewed on TV about a big deer he had bagged. In Arkansas, deer season is Christmas for adults. The kids benefit as well because there is no school on the first day of the season. How is such a massive, statewide slaughter given so much credence and latitude? Easy… respect. As the orange-capped fellow described the big kill, he started using words that I, a recent convert to environmental causes, found comforting. "For me, deer hunting is all about getting back to nature. You know, being one with nature. I'm just thankful that god blessed me with the opportunity to kill such an amazing animal. I respect these animals so much because of their speed and ability to survive, they really are something. So, really, I just want to give God the glory for this. I'm humbled by being fortunate enough to kill this record breaking deer."

Interesting. If the concept is true, we should be able to apply it to other things we respect. Such as, "For me, cousin hunting is all about getting back to family. You know, being one with family. I'm just thankful that God blessed me with the opportunity to kill such an amazing cousin. I respect these family members so much because of their speed and ability to survive reunions, they really are something. So, really, I just want to give God the glory for this. I'm humbled by being fortunate enough to kill this record breaking cousin." I'll have to do some research but I think there were a couple of dudes in the 90's that got in trouble for killing people they wanted to be at one with. It's all terribly confusing.

While working at a girl's camp in Maine, I learned archery from one of the all-time greats, Art Hall. I had taught archery before and thought I was a decent practitioner but Mr. Hall was able to refine my bare-bow technique to an unbelievable degree. After completing the course, I went back to camp and began practicing on the range before the campers arrived. It wasn't long before I could tag any section on the twenty-yard targets. Thirty, forty, and even fifty-yard targets were mastered within a few days. With a few arrows left in my quiver at the end of the day, I raised my bow and focused down the range. Suddenly, I was distracted by a brown, fury mass scuttling along the back of the range. It was probably close to sixty-five yards out. "I wonder…no. That was the old me. I've changed."

A few weeks later, while enjoying a weekend jaunt to Portland, the city of discount shopping centers, I was in a hunting store looking over the archery gear. My interest in the sport was growing and my skill level had me searching for greater challenges all the time. My latest trick was shooting a soda can off of a ten-yard target and nailing it to the bull's eye on the twenty yard target. Sweet!

As I made my way through the store, my attention was drawn to a hunting video playing next to a display of tree stands. The hunter was hunkered down in nervous excitement. His eager eyes darted back and forth from the camera to the edge of the woods as he whispered his giddy commentary, "Can you see him? Right over there! Trash dumps are a great place to hunt for bears. They come here to forage and dig through the garbage. Most of the local bears probably swing by here every day. There he is! Oh, man. Oh, man." He stealthily raised himself to one knee and took aim. The arrow zipped away and an instant later, the bear ran. "Wait. I know I hit him. Wait. Listen…there it is! Hear that? Can you hear it? That's the death groan! Come on!" The video then cut to the elated hunter standing over a large black bear. "Look at him! Wow! He is awesome. I'll tell you what. This is some special bear. Look at his nose. See all those scratches and scars. This bear is a warrior. He's probably been ruling this region for years. Man, he is something. What a special creature!" It was clear to me that this hunter had a great amount of respect for the bear.

By pure coincidence, that very bear was the subject of another locale wildlife documentary and was wearing a microphone at the time of the incident. The following is the transcript of that fateful day: "I can't believe these idiots have me up so early. My feet are killing me. I haven't slept well in a stinking week. Let's see…fish or rubbish? That water is gonna be ass cold. Rubbish it is. (Ten minutes of walking with no talk.)   What was that? Hello? Sound guy? Who's there? Anyone? I hate this place. (Eight minutes of walking with no talk.) Ohhhh. Yeah! That was a good one. Did you get that camera man? Did you get that? Ohho, man, I feel much better now. Well, I guess I just answered that age old question, huh? Yeah! (Three minutes walking sounds, no talk.) Finally, jeez. Wow, first one here. I smell…(sniffing)… what is that? Pastrami? I hope that's pastrami. Okay, here goes the wild bear scavenging for food. Maybe I'll growl, that'll be cool. I'll eat first. Then I'll growl. Oh, a cupcake. Holy sweetness. (Zipping sound.) Ow! What the fuck?! What was that? Hey, sound guy, I think my microphone shocked me. Holy shit, that hurts! What the…I'm bleeding! Hey, somebody, the bear is bleeding. Is that an arrow? Seriously, someone, is this an arrow? I'm getting light headed. Cut. Can we cut? I need to lie down. Oh, shit, this is really hurting. I'm getting…dizzy…must run…away. (Limping, running noises with heavy breathing.) I can't go on. (Yelling.) Bear down! The bear is down! Ohhhhhhhh! Ohhhhhhhhhh! Who's that…can't focus…maybe that nice man with the funny hat will help me. (End transcription.)

Seeing the absurdity of the hunt made me realize how asinine killing for pleasure really is. I felt like I had been healed. The need to kill, to showcase my manly skills, had subsided as maturity set in. Killing things wasn't such a hard habit to break after all – or so I thought. One of the biggest challenges that alcoholics face is their well intended friends offering spirits to relax or celebrate. Recovering killers face the same type of trials.

While attending grad school at the University of Oklahoma, I was befriended by a strange looking fellow who embodied all that is Oklahoma with a peppering of Texas heritage for additional cultural flavoring. Deon was a lanky dude with a terminally tilted head, jutting elbows, starched jeans and a collection of Southwestern inspired button-downs that would make Sam Elliot smile. One hundred and fifty years ago, Deon would have been a successful cattle mogul, but modern times forced his kind to drive a Cadillac and sing country/western songs. I shudder to think of the implications, but we were instant friends. After a long semester of working on a couple of difficult projects, Deon invited me to go to Texas for the weekend where we would do nothing but relax. After promising that I would experience a life-changing getaway, he made one simple suggestion, "You should bring your bow."

Our destination was about eighty miles East of Lubbock, Texas on a privately owned ranch. We drove past the main house toward a cabin nestled in the midst of an oak grove at the edge of small lake. It was actually an oversized pond but Texans like things big and a small lake implied more size and grandeur than a big pond. Regardless, it was as serene as it was isolated with lush greenery and an abundance of deer and rabbit. Deon's Pawpaw (That's Texan for Grandfather.) met us at the cabin and was kind enough to take us on a pickup tour of the property. Just before we piled in the back, Deon made a simple suggestion, "You should bring your bow."

Not many people travel with a bow, so Pawpaw's questions were certainly understandable. I had been mistaken for a hunter, which I wasn't. I explained that I was simply a target shooter and enjoyed the challenge offered by the bow and arrow. As the old truck rattled and bumped along the washed out dirt road, Deon saw an opportunity for some fun and shouted for Pawpaw to stop the truck. "Betcha cain't hit that rabbit!" About twenty yards from the road, a brown jackrabbit sat perfectly still, probably wondering why a truckload of people had stopped. Pawpaw eyeballed the distance and quickly confirmed Deon's assessment. "That'd be an awfully pretty tough shot with a bow." Actually, it wasn't.

I drew back the arrow until the nock was just touching the right corner of my mouth. "Damn rabbit. Why'd you have to stop there? Run, you moron." Suddenly, I realized that since Pawpaw had his doubts about the shot, there would be no shame in missing. I could simply lob a shot right over little bunny's noggin, and we could all get excited about how close I was. Everybody wins. Deep breath, steady…zing!

There's an oddity in archery called The Archer's Paradox. As an arrow flies, it contorts in an almost oblong fashion similar to a spinning jump rope moving at 120 mph. Of course, I can't blame the Archer's Paradox for what happened next, but I can say that I had no intention of hitting the rabbit and certainly didn't plan on shooting an arrow through both of its ears. Poor little, bastard rabbit.

Understandably, Pawpaw and Deon winced at the ear piercing. I was glad the bunny got away, but I suddenly felt a surge of embarrassment by the miss, as well as the subsequent maiming, of course. I would only have to wait about eight hours to redeem myself…if a monumental moment of regret can qualify as redemption.

About fifty years ago, one of Deon's ancestors made a unique contribution to this country. Erosion had been a problem along many riverbanks and, before the machinery was available to dredge some of the major water systems and slow the flow, a lot of land was lost. Kudzu, also known as the Vine That Ate The South, was brought in and planted to take care of the eroding riverbanks. Who could have guessed that this hardy plant would spread so quickly that it became a bigger problem than erosion? Enter Deon's great-great-something-or-another. To battle the foreign plant, he brought in a foreign critter that snacks on kudzu, the nutria. Imagine a rat with the body and head of a beaver and a thick whip-like tail. The Viet Nam rodent reproduced at a plague-like pace and soon, of course, became a bigger problem than the kudzu. Ironically, the nutria dug so many holes in riverbanks that erosion was, once again, a big concern. While some people (Louisianans) eat the nasty vermin, Texans use them for target practice.

It was about eleven o'clock at night and Pawpaw had long since headed back home. Deon and I had been drinking when he had a great idea to go out in the boat. It's important to keep in mind how creepy large, overgrown ponds are at night, especially when water moccasins and copper heads are abundant. Silence never quite takes over due to so many scurrying, diving noises that are difficult to identify after a few beers. Deon knew the pond was being overrun with nutria and made an innocent suggestion, "You should bring your bow."

We had two flashlights but didn't dare use them unless absolutely necessary as the mosquitoes would instantly form a biting fog whenever the light came on. The thought of an alligator tipping the boat over was foremost in my mind, even though the nearest alligator was probably about 200 hundred miles away. The next thought in line was that I would have to kill a stupid rat. Finally, I came up with the perfect excuse, "Deon, these arrows are expensive. Even if I hit one of those nasty things, I'll probably lose my arrow." Deon took an arrow from the quiver and placed it in the water. "It floats. Don't be such a tight ass. I'll buy you another one."

We moved as silently through the water as possible but couldn't help frightening monstrous bullfrogs that were about as graceful as a crowbar with their belly-flopping splashes. Finally, Deon's flashlight caught a reflection moving a little more than an inch above the water. It was the dreaded nutria, awkwardly dog-paddling across the pond. Deon stirred quickly to get my attention, causing the water rat to dive. Whew. I was so relieved at how skittish these butt-ugly animals truly were that I drank another beer.

Deon dialed back the focus on the flashlight to throw a wider, but less intense beam across the surface. It was only about a minute later that another target presented itself. With only the nose and part of the head sticking out of the water, the rodent didn't offer much of a shot. It was here that I unknowingly made the transition from regret to intrigue. Could I actually hit one of these damn things? After all, the target area was tiny and the body of the animal was below the surface. There was a decent chance the arrow would simply skip off the surface. I drew back the arrow as the animal continued swimming parallel to the boat about twenty yards out. As soon as I had full extension, I realized a problem with bow hunting at night. Typically, bow hunters use the string and the arrow as sights to line up with the target, but at nighttime, this was nearly impossible.

I decided that shooting at the head was a waste of time and would certainly lead to a lost arrow. The best chance was to aim behind the head and down a few inches, hoping to hit the neck or body. Deep breath, steady…zing! Damn. The nutria disappeared. "Oh! That was so close!" exclaimed a giddy Deon. "Shit. I lost the arrow. Dude, seriously, I only have about ten of these. I have to order them from Maine." He talked me into shooting a few more, and I talked him into to paddling around in hopes of recovering some of my losses.

We searched and searched and didn't find one stinking arrow…until…we found one stinking arrow. Deon spotted it first, "Over there." It was certainly one my arrows but exactly what it was doing was a mystery. Near a thicket of cattails, the arrow was slowly swaying back and forth. "What the heck?" It didn't make any sense. It was as if the arrow had somehow embedded itself in a log that was being gently rocked back and forth by the water. As the boat slowly glided closer, the mystery become painfully clear as two little feet pawed at the surface and a tiny nose came up for air. "Oh, shit. Are you kidding me? Oh, for the love…!" My hard earned buzz dried up as remorse rained down.

The good news is that my calculations were dead on. The arrow had, indeed, hit the nutria right in the throat. The bad news is that the arrow had hit the animal right in the throat and now the little shit was swimming around looking about as sad and pathetic as an animal could look. Deon and I exchanged embarrassed looks of deep regret. Despicable. Deplorable. Down right shameful. Damn me!

That fateful arrow was shot roughly thirteen years ago and to this day I vividly remember seeing that little fucker pirouetting for its life, trying to keep its pointy snout above water. I can only image his inner monologue and the meeting of senior members of the nutria community to discuss measures against similar attacks. So why all the regret and shame over such a shitty animal? I killed hundreds of birds, a couple of squirrels, a woodchuck, fish, frogs, snakes and who knows what else. But this one had an impact. Why? It didn't die. Death is permanent. When death happens, that's it, the story ends. Death is the last chapter. There's no pain, no squirming, nothing. It's hard to feel sorry for something inanimate and death makes all things inanimate. But that one little scrapper didn't die. He fought. He struggled. He won.

I put down my bow, never to hunt again. It was a hard lesson learned, but I was left with a true respect for all living creatures, unlike those heartless hunters who claim to kill because they love animals. Hypocrites! I was, at last, cured of cruelty. To spread the word and do more for animals, to stop the insanity, to put an end to senseless killing, I will soon be funding an awareness program that will one day defeat the hunting movement.

Using my real-life experience as inspiration, my system will foster kindness and compassion by encouraging hunters to wound animals rather than kill them, forcing them to feel the same dread that has haunted me for so long. It's not an end-all solution, but it is a start. If you love animals as much as I do, call 1-800-MAIM-4-LIFE. Together, we can make a difference.

MY GREATEST HITS

With the exception of horror movies, I can't think of anything that's ever scared me. Eating cookie dough, riding in elevators, driving without a seatbelt…danger makes me laugh. However, every Superman has his Kryptonite just like every politician has a secret lover with an incriminating photo of a drunken moment of ecstasy. For me, that one silver bullet is singing. Public speaking…no problem, put me in the middle of a packed Superdome and I'll talk all day. Ask me to carry a note and there's a damn decent chance that I'll stop breathing and fall on my gourd. Simply put, the act of singing terrifies the living poop out of me. I'm being completely literal here. If you were to put a gun to my head and force me to sing, my poop would run out of ass as fast as possible, screaming at the top of its little poop lungs, looking for a safe place to hide. This story is about conquering a fear only to have it return in less than three minutes. It's also a story that perfectly illustrates the power of motivation and the lasting effects of harsh criticism. Reader beware…it ain't pretty.

It was my second year to work at a Christian summer camp in the hill country of Texas and I had been promoted from counselor to assistant activities director.

Most of my days were spent planning large format games for eighty to one hundred campers or prepping for sketch comedy routines based on the weeks' theme such as jungle, spy, or the American Revolution. The previous summer had been, and still remains to this day, one of the best summers of my life. This second summer was well on its way to being a fantastic sequel.

One of the staff members that I worked closely with was the music director, a lovely woman whom I shall refer to as Angel. Of course, her name wasn't Angel, but she was one of the nicest, most gracious, encouraging, loving individuals I have ever known. I must also mention that she made the best damn steak I've ever eaten. I'm not kidding. She cooked a steak for me that was a heavenly slice of… (deep breath in honor of a fond memory)…seriously, it was good. One afternoon I was hanging out with Angel in the chapel when she commented that I had a nice voice. She then asked me if I ever sang. "No. No. Not me. Never…I wish."

Angel, perplexed by my certainty that I could not sing, matter-of-factly stated, "If you want to sing, why don't you sing?" She laughed when I told her how nervous it made me to even think about singing. Keep in mind that she, over the course of two summers, had seen me perform countless voluntary acts of embarrassment to entertain the campers. It was a gift. In her mind, singing was a simple task that anyone could perform. Finally, I told her that I would love to sing and had even thought of trying a song that was more speaking than singing. "Perfect!" A smile spread across her face at the thought, "I'll work with you. It will be fun."

I don't know what became of the pop-Christian singer Carman, but back in eighties, he was a hugely popular entertainer. His songs were full of passion and an operatic quality that was as moving as anything I'd ever heard. A recent revisit of his music sounded super cheesy, but, during that summer, it was all the Christian rage. My selection was a narrative called Jericho. It was based on the biblical story about the heavily fortified walls surrounding the ancient city of Jericho and how faith caused those mighty walls to come tumbling down. The point of the song was that, with faith, we could all bring down the walls of our personal Jericho. I practiced the song everyday for at least two weeks. At the end of each rehearsal, Angel would smile and nod. I couldn't believe how such a deeply felt fear was quickly melting away.

The big day came, and I felt as though I was about to bungee jump from a low flying helicopter. Angel introduced me to a chapel full of kids who all knew me. She handed me the microphone, walked over to the tape deck and pushed play. I could feel my voice tense as I began and I was immediately reminded of how terrified I had always been of this moment. In the brief nanosecond before panic swept over me, I glanced down at the campers and made a comforting realization...every kid in the building had confidence in me. No one was cringing or covering their eyes or cramming their fingers in their ears. These were kids that I constantly joked with and encouraged on a daily basis. We had a relationship and part of that relationship was trust. As they looked at me, I suddenly understood that the thought of me failing had never entered their young minds. They were simply trusting that I was, as always, sharing something with them that was important to me. That faith and trust flattened my brief wave of panic and allowed me to do something I never thought possible.

I'm certain that if a video of my performance actually exists, it would be terrible. Even as I type, my memory of the event is tainted by my fear of having to watch it some day. I shudder to imagine what I must have sounded like.

The performance may have been awful, but the moment was incredible. The song ended with a huge build up that asked the audience to stand and shout. They did and we all celebrated the idea of triumph, of tumbling the walls of doubt. We had all shared a moment of encouragement. I do not have the words, nor do I believe they exist, to explain the feeling of sheer joy that those kids were kind enough to bestow upon me. It was a feeling that lasted for nearly three minutes.

As soon as the song was over, I was so amped up that I had to leave the building to settle down. Fifty yards from the chapel, I sat in the shade under a tree and began to relax for the first time in days. A moment later, another counselor walked up with a perplexed look, "Dude, that's messed up. I'm so sorry."

What ever could he be referring to? I was sitting on a cloud under an oak tree at one with the world. "What do you mean?" I said with a smile of encouragement. His concern grew as he realized he was the bearer of F'd up news, "Oh, you don't know…?"

Imagine you are about to jump from one skyscraper to the next. Your heart races as you sprint down the runway and you take the leap of your life. The rush of cold air pushes you back as the reality of failure flashes before your eyes. Rather than relax and enjoy the free-fall, you stretch as far as you can until your feet land atop the next building. You stand thinking, "Holy crap! I made it. I can't believe I made it!" As you take it all in, someone strolls up and says, "Too bad you fell to your death. Nice try, though."

As I had walked out of the chapel, the next person to take the microphone was Brother Glenn. BG was the camp director and one of the inspirational leaders of the entire organization. Years ago he had been a college football star. On a fateful, drunken drive back to campus, he wrecked his car and lost the use of his legs. Confined to a wheel chair, he decided to give the rest of his body to Jesus and was now a bona fide, born-again believer.

BG hushed the kids and told them to ignore the performance they were currently celebrating. He explained that music and emotion are a dangerous combination and that the song I had performed was a type of emotional and mental manipulation that was used to brainwash young people.

Imagine my shock to find out that I had attempted to brainwash the campers. I wondered what my motive could have been. Was it something sinister? Perhaps I was going to rally the children to go to war or get them to protest outside of an abortion clinic. What ever I had in mind must have been terrible and disaster was surely upon us all.

Later, Angel tried her best to explain BG's well-intended lesson. She was clearly as dumbfounded as I and was being forced to play nicey-nice. I nodded as she tried to comfort me but knew I had to approach BG for further spiritual guidance and understanding of my sin.

BG rolled into his living room with a bible on his lap. He gave a disappointing look and justified the public reprimand with, "Jesus never sang."

"Excuse me?"

He pushed his glasses a little further up his nose and then picked up his left leg, placing over his right leg to assume more of a professor like position. "Jesus never sang." He looked at me as if the explanation needed no further comment. I was trumped. I had no comeback. Regardless of the fact that songs were sung in the chapel three times a day, my song was apparently the type of music that Jesus would not have approved. How could I argue? I wanted to come up with an example of Jesus singing but I was being bombarded by images of all of the other horrible things that I had done that Jesus never did: playing basketball, driving a car, riding a horse, eating a cheese burger, seeing a movie, flushing a toilet, squeezing a boob. I was in deep doody.

Religious guidance is a valuable and priceless necessity in life. I was lucky enough to have someone present to help point me back to the path of righteousness. It was the type of spiritual lesson that opened my eyes to the world around me. I was suddenly aware of the dangerous, hedonistic snares laid by Satan to make the good man stumble. Thanks to BG, I could see clearly through the fog of temptation and secular misgivings. There was only one road to redemption; I reclaimed my fear of singing to ensure that I would never stray again, at least not any time soon.

Fifteen years later, in lovely Burbank, California, I sat in a bar with my teammates as we celebrated winning the city league basketball championship for guys that used to be athletes. My wife was home with our new baby, so I knew I couldn't stay too long. Besides, Thursday was karaoke night so the place was pretty loud and rowdy, not the type of environment I find relaxing. I tried to leave but was forced to have a shot of tequila. Three shots later, someone decided to purchase a bottle of Patron, the expensive, yet ultra-smooth, top-shelf tequila. With the entire team doing shots, the establishment quickly ran out of shot glasses. I thought it was odd that tumblers were placed on the table to facilitate our drinking needs, but what the heck, I was about to leave anyway. I didn't immediately realize that double-shots were being poured into the tumblers so, with approximately fifteen shots racing through my bloodstream, I experienced a brief memory lapse. Sadly, it's impossible to explain what happens during a memory lapse, however, just beyond the blank spot, I have an extremely vivid memory.

When my vision returned, I had trouble seeing due to the bright lights shining in my face. Squinting ahead, I noticed that everyone in the bar was looking at me. They were also singing and swaying and having a good time. My hearing returned and I realized I was listening to Garth Brookes' Friends in Low Places. But the voice…that voice… it wasn't Garth. Who was that singing? It sounds so familiar.

It was me. I was sitting on a barstool in front of a microphone singing. I started leaning precariously to the left when I felt a hand steady me. Still singing, I turned to my right and realized I was singing a duet with a sixty-something-year-old woman who was apparently my new best friend. We were a hit.

With the echo of applause still ringing in my ear, I walked to my car wondering whether or not I was too drunk to drive. Knowing I wasn't really in the frame of mind to be making life and death decisions, I quickly concocted a sobriety test to guard against the altered mind of imagined immortality. Rather than the standard walking of a straight line, I decided to jog down the street and back. No staggering, no tripping, no problem. I was further encouraged by the fact that it only took three times to get my key in the car door.

As I pulled the sedan door open, I began thinking of BG and the lesson he had taught me. I wondered how disappointed he would have been to see me singing to a bar full of vulnerable minds and social outcasts. I pictured him sitting in an oversized, tricked-out wheel chair with a cow skull as a front grill ornament and shellacked, Texas-sized scorpions spinning in the center of each wheel. His head shook with frustration as he pointed to his bible and reminded me of the things Jesus never did. "You know, my son, Jesus never karaoked and, according the Gospel of Mark, never, ever did shots of Patron." The line between drunken hallucination and bizarre reality blurred as BG squinted intensely and bunny hopped his whip even closer.

I stepped back as sadness and shame began to overcome me. A remorseful tear began to form in my eye as my shoulders dropped and my bottom lip quivered. BG aggressively flipped to the book of Corinthians to punctuate his upcoming sermon in the street. I was slowly shrinking into nothingness when I made a startling realization...this smug little, know-it-all, pious, pompous, pain in the ass vision of BG was totally killing my tequila buzz.

I walked behind BG's glowing image, ignoring his zealous spouting about Judas of Iscariot, and placed my hands on the chair's handles. The front wheels lifted as I tilted him back and took a couple of quick steps toward the curb. BG nearly bounced out of the chair as he crashed through the saloon doors and spun out on the sawdust and peanut shell covered floor. Someone, I can't say for certain who, yelled out, "What the fuck!"

Satisfied that I had finally banished that belligerent, Baptist banshee, I shoved my keys in my pocket and smiled as I staggered home singing every song I could think of for the next three miles.

THE BONE YARD

For as far back as I can remember, every visit to my Grandfather's house meant playing at least a couple of games of dominoes. If there was no one to play with, Mr. Solitaire, or Ol' Sol as Grandpa called him, was always ready for another round. Dominoes is one of the simplest games ever devised, if the pieces on the end total a number divisible by five, you've scored. Of course, there are countless strategies that Grandpa would never share with me that I'm only now beginning to understand. I always looked forward to playing with him even with the thick blanket of cigarette smoke that hung like ominous rain clouds in the room. It was just he and I, and that was always fine by me.

After about our thousandth game, I started wondering how he could play as many games as he did. He must have played twenty or more games every day. Sometimes he would drive to the nearby town of Mulberry to play at a domino hall. Even when his eyes went bad, he played on. Macular degeneration took most of his sight, leaving him with only periphery vision and no ability to see straight ahead. He would cock his head sideways and lean down to get a better view of his choices. Still, his disadvantage rarely translated to an advantage for me. My best streak was winning three in a row, but I seldom ever won more than four out of ten. His favorite strategy was to "sew 'em up." This meant that his opponent had no choices in their hand and had to draw. Somehow, he always knew, before I did, that I couldn't play. "Get in that bone yard!" The bone yard was the pile of dominos from which you would draw when you couldn't play. I suppose the name comes from the resemblance of the pile of face down ivory pieces to tombstones in a graveyard. After drawing every last domino, the play went to Grandpa who now knew exactly what was in my hand, which meant that I would probably not get another turn.

As much as I loved playing with him, there was nothing more frustrating. "Better play that double six now or you won't get a chance later." He was always right about that one. I still hate that damn double six. Every warning filtered through a puff of smoke and a confident, slow, scratchy voice that made it impossible to tell whether or not he really knew what I had – which he always did. He had a great phrase for every play. With a big score he would smile, "Now I've got you where the hair is short." It took me about ten years to figure that one out. If I scored a measly five points he would shake his head in disappointment, "I can't believe you'd stoop for a nickel." After five or six games, I would start to get bored of all the losing. How could he possibly play for so many years? Yes, he was a great player, but it's such a simple game.

It's been over ten years since Grandpa died. Today, I have one friend that will play dominos with me. Our games usually consist of a lot of drinking and a lot of laughing. Having renewed my own interest in dominos, I think I've come to understand why he loved the game, and it has nothing to do with the game itself. I think it has to do with thoughts. Thoughts that give birth to questions, thoughts that won't go away, and even thoughts that are so dear that you need to look busy so no one interrupts the moment. When he played with friends or grandkids, I think he truly enjoyed the company and focused on the person as much as he did the game. But when he played Sol, I think there was something else going on. I think the joking and the razor sharp one-liners were replaced with deeper internal conversations about his life and the questions that he must have pondered each day and wrestled with each night.

I once asked Grandpa what he would have been if he could do it all over again. I expected to hear him say that he would have stayed in school, gone to college, or been a baseball player. He told me wanted to open up a scrap yard. He always wanted to own a scrap yard. But as simple as his dream was, his real life was as complicated, painful, and as joyous as any life ever lived.

Born in 1912, Samuel Jackson Nixon was one of eight children. I always called him Grandpa but his friends called him "Bo." In 1918, the Southern states were hit with a devastating outbreak of the Spanish flu. Bo's mother became deathly ill and fell into a coma-like state of unconsciousness. While she hovered precariously between life and death, three of her children succumbed to the virus. Her miraculous recovery left little to celebrate as she discovered a loss that no parent should have to endure.

A few weeks later, Bo and his siblings came home after school to find the doors locked. They waited outside until their dad arrived and kicked the door in. Moments later, Bo's mother was found dead with a self-inflicted gunshot wound. I imagine that the world became terribly silent as he searched for answers, trying to comprehend life without his mother and why she would chose to leave him.

A few years later, during a thunderstorm, young Bo became frightened and went to sleep with his dad. The next day, the storm had passed and so had his father. A heart attack in the night left an eleven-year old Bo to wonder why God would take his only parent, his only protector.

Bo and his siblings were divided among family and strangers gracious enough to help a shattered family. Money was scarce as the country was ramping up for the Great Depression so most of the work that a young boy could find was paid in food and shelter, which was, more often than not, a couple of eggs and a cot in a storage room. Roughly seventy years later, Bo still struggled with the choices he was forced to make as a matter of survival. "I stole if I had to, but only when I was going hungry."

During his difficult youth, Bo was exposed to a multitude of people. Some were good, and some were bad. The most damaging of all seemed to be the Baptist preacher. Even in his later years, Bo struggled with the idea of being a sinner. He had been told a thousand times that his soul needed salvation and seemed to believe that, somehow, the awful circumstances of his younger days were his fault.

Of all the stories I've heard about the early days, there was one bright spot that he retold with a smile. While climbing a pecan tree with his brother William, he saw a pretty young girl walking with her mother. Bo was a seventh grade drop out who, at this point in his life, had suffered more than most people can imagine. It's no wonder that a little girl walking with her mother would be an image of such beauty that he stopped "monkeying" around to simply stare. As the story goes, Bo turned to his brother and stated with full confidence, "I'm gonna marry that girl." Eight years later, he did.

Bo and Laura Bell's new life together was anything but easy. However, for a boy who had experienced nothing but pain and instability, having the woman of his dreams to come home to, life was certainly on an upswing. Seeing the first of his ten babies born, Bo must have experienced a bit of a rebirth himself. All at once, he was part of a complete family.

At the age of thirty-four, with six kids to feed, Bo was drafted into World War II. Having two daughters of my own, the thought of being drafted makes me panic. For Bo, it was a steady paycheck with benefits. He carried two pictures with him as he traveled around Europe, one of his young wife, Laura Bell, and a group shot of his children. One of the few photos that he sent back from the war was of him smiling, holding the two photos near his face.

As the war raged on, Bo's primary concern was his family back in the states. He sent money as often as he got it and even polished officer's shoes to earn extra cash. Despite all of the hardships that he had endured, Bo was one of the most soft-hearted persons alive. He never met a stranger, and anyone willing to spend time with him was an instant family member. While stationed in Paris, he befriended a man who admired him because he had a large family. Knowing what it was like to not have a family; Bo must have felt some sort of connection with this lonely soldier. One night, while everyone else had gone to local taverns, Bo polished the last of the shoes and sat down to write a letter to Laura Bell. His new friend commented that he wished he had a family to write home to. Bo handed him a piece of paper and a pencil, "You can write to mine."

Bo survived his World War II duties and was thankful that he never had to kill anyone. Having gained no valuable skill in the military, he made a living with his hands and back. He took a job with the highway department, but, with so many kids, had to find other ways to supplement his income. With a pickup truck and a chainsaw, Bo made ends meet by trimming trees. "See those shoes up that tree? I'm gonna go up there and get those shoes for you." When a need arose, be it new shoes or clothes, it was always up in a tree, and Bo would work extra hours to get it down.

Working so many hours, Bo had no time for fishing, camping, or vacations. His only outlet for anxiety was a pack of cigarettes a day and a tall "Bud". Being slight of frame, it didn't take much for Bo to get drunk. The kids could always tell if it was going to be a good night or a bad night the moment their daddy got home. If the truck rolled too far forward and bumped into the porch, it was time to run and hide because Bo was "in a mood."

Of all the tough years that Bo survived, 1968 must have been the most challenging. An accident at work left him with a shattered foot and unable to earn money for his ever-growing family. What little belongings his family had, were destroyed in a fire that burned their home to nothing more than a charred foundation. It's difficult to image what an already suffering family must have felt like when the Army informed them that one of their four sons serving in Viet Nam had been killed in combat. The tragic and devastating loss was repeated only a few short weeks later when another son took it upon himself to hold back an advancing enemy while his comrades escaped a dangerous ravine.

As difficult as Bo's life was, there are two moments that make a case for a triumphant existence. Bo and Laura's fiftieth wedding anniversary took place in and an old gymnasium. The building was erected after the Great Depression and was meant to generate a stronger sense of community. At the end of the basketball court was a stage for plays, public speaking, performances, etc. On this particular day, over one hundred people, including family, grandkids, great-grandkids, and close friends had gathered to celebrate a marriage that had seen and survived all that life could throw at it. I remember standing on one end of the gym and looking across a sea of people to see my grandfather taking it all in. Sixty-some-odd years earlier, Bo had been a hopeless, scared little boy swamped with loneliness and despair. Now, he was a king.

Not long after my grandparents' sixtieth wedding anniversary, Laura Bell died of cancer at the age of 76. Bo outlived his beloved wife by three years. He refused to live with any of his children, despite being blind and hard of hearing. At the age of 85, his mind was a sharp as ever and he had only recently given up trying to feel the black dots on domino pieces. When cancer came for Bo, it hit him hard and fast. In a few short months, his chronic cough became a debilitating struggle to breath against the fluid that was drowning him. His last day of living arrived with some warning. Calls went out and his children gathered to say good-bye and send him off with loving assurances. As he lay in his bed, my mom told him that everyone but Glenda had arrived. With his limited hearing, Bo thought he heard, "Everyone is here." He nodded and said, "Alright, well, I'm gonna go then." Mom's eyes widened with panic, "No! No! Glenda's NOT here." Bo nodded, "Alright, I'll wait."

A short time later, as all of his children sat talking softly to each other, Bo placed his hands behind his head and slipped quietly to the other side surrounded by a family that loved him dearly.

Looking at any one moment of Bo's life could lead one to believe that he lived a life of suffering and sadness, of unfathomable loss and constant heartache. But no puzzle is complete without all of the pieces, especially the last one. Bo's story is one of great endurance, of overcoming tragedy with the hope of a better day. The lessons he taught me were simple: you only lose if you stop playing and always, no matter what, get rid of that damn double six as soon as you can.

PREACHER GETS A HUMMER

Not long ago, I had to take an emergency trip back home. My mother had sold her house in the country and was moving back to the comforts of the big city. Mom is a tough broad and there are many people in town who have been bested by my favorite super-hero over the years, but moving an ass-load of heavy furniture was her kryptonite.

It was my first time back in town in almost three years, and I was immediately confronted with the fact that this was a dying community. Wal-Mart had already kicked downtown in the stomach and only a few antique shops and a diner remained. Students no longer cruised the streets on weekends. As a matter of fact, it was difficult to even tell where the main strip was. Each road was as desolate as the next. There was only one new building in the entire town. An enormous new church just as you drive in from the East bound 64 hwy. I heard all kinds of rumors from many different types of people but the one story that really got me going was the tawdry rumor of a preacher getting a hummer. Does juicier content exist? Of course not! Preacher, hummer? Hummer, preacher? A humble servant of the Lord!!! What's up with that?

Here's a good place for some historical perspective. Allow me to take you on a quick tour of the religious community of a town of 3,000 people. We'll start in 1980 and quickly get to the naughty hummer of 2005. With the exception of being forced to go to my grandmother's Pentecostal church every Easter, I first became a legitimate church member (meaning baptized in water) around 1980 when my bus driver invited me to his church, that is, the church where he moonlit as a preacher.

The sleepy little church was just around the corner from my trailer and by cutting through the woods, I could be there in less than five minutes. The preacher-man was a good guy and showed an immediate interest in me. Having only an invisible step-dad and a stepbrother, who had fled to California to be with his mom, I really didn't have anyone else with whom I could pass the slow ticks of summer days. Of the four years that I attended this quaint little church, three memories stand out above all others.

1) In the middle of a Sunday sermon, we heard Brother George's wife scream from their house next door. Being pregnant and having other kids to care for, she had stayed home that day. Someone rushed in and whispered in Brother George's ear and then both men raced away. A moment later, we heard a loud and furious booming noise. The large copperhead snake that had snuck into the pastor's home had been discovered and dismembered with an axe. Brother George returned a few moments later and finished his lesson about John the Baptist.

2) Sunday school started at 10:00 am each Sunday morning and was a series of lessons for every age. I was with the young adult group: 13 – 18 years old. There were three people in the class. This lesson was being taught by Sister Terri, Brother George's wife. We had just finished the story of Cain and Abel when Terri informed us that black people came about as a punishment for Cain killing his brother, Abel. God gave him the mark of a murderer, which apparently was being turned black. The other students nodded their heads as if to say, "I see. Interesting." But I was smarter than the other students and my cerebral wheels were

spinning (I should note that I was a basketball player and had dreams of a college scholarship). There weren't many people of color in my region, so all I knew of them was that they were a little taller, could usually jump a little higher, and were typically quicker. I looked across the room at Donny Ed, an annoying brat whose gray matter hit capacity two years earlier, and squinted my eyes as a plan formed. If I killed Donny Ed, God would strike me black! I could increase my vertical jump by at least four inches and get immediate street cred. Could a free ride to the U of A be this easy? I soon learned that God's law and man's law didn't always agree and that there could be a more severe penalty than a simple pigment makeover. I never actually killed Donny Ed, but I've always thought I would have had a stellar college career if I could have just jumped this much higher.

3) Wayne, the ultimate goofball, happened to be present for the final memory of 52 South Highway Baptist Church. I should warn readers that this next memory is utterly and absolutely disgusting. If you have a strong gag reflex, move on to the next story or at least be responsible enough to not read this in a Starbucks. Here we go… Wayne and I were sitting in a pew, bored out of our skulls during a hot, humid, Sunday morning while five old ladies, trying to out squall each other, were butchering a hymn. This was a special Sunday because the Tetter family had joined the congregation. The Tetters, seven total, always arrived in a small Toyota pickup, Rory drove with his mother and his mail-order bride in the front. In the back, despite the weather, rode Uncle Marlan, and three siblings – Tess Mae, Deltry, and, the youngest, Ronchy. All the Tetters spoke in a breathy stop-plosive manner that I could not begin to convey without the talents of Billy Bob Thornton and Bobby McFerrin. As far as I know, the Tetters were the only successful family in the battle against running water and indoor toilets. They were built like flagpoles, with hair that shined from the natural body oils produced by hard work and hot summers. There was no sleeve known to man that could reach the wrist of a Tetter. They were long like the closing shots of Sergio Leone western.

Here's the moment: The church was already hot and ripe with Tetter waft, and Wayne and I were dizzy from a lack of clean oxygen and the eighth verse of Brother Nester's favorite hymn. Just then, Rory Tetter, who was not singing, but looking at the open hymnal as if he were fascinated by the letters and lines, sneezed. He made no effort to hide or suppress this explosion. There was no build up and no warning. This was a dirty-bomb blast. Wayne and I jolted and turned our unexpected eyes toward the oldest Tetter. What we saw haunts us to this day and binds us in a way that only friends who have shared a tragedy can truly understand. Spanning the roughly eighteen-inch distance between Rory's hymnal and the tip of his nose was a yellow-green rope of snot. My first thought was to call 911 because I thought he had been shot in the back of the head causing his brains to spill. Unfortunately, it was much worse. Poor Rory must have been in shock as well. Possibly, he was dizzy from having lost so much body weight in such a short amount of time. Regardless, he sat motionless for a least fifteen seconds, the only exception was his eyes darting back and forth searching the congregation for witnesses. Wayne and I were two pews back and to the left…back and to the left…too astonished to move, too flabbergasted to laugh. Certain that no one was wise to him, Rory slowly moved the ill-fated book of song toward his nose …and closed it. He then placed the book back in its holder and leaned back as if nothing had happened.

A crime had been committed and only three people knew about it. I don't know how Rory sleeps, but I still jolt upright in the middle of the night from visions of some poor Baptist bastard, wanting to praise God with voice and good cheer, opening that damn hymnal and wondering who in the hell would have left a fish in a song book.

I'm not very familiar with many of the other churches in town, but I do remember a Methodist preacher playing tennis and dropping an F-bomb as his ball sailed out of bounds. When I was in junior high, the Second Baptist church (Was it Second or Third Baptist Church? I know it wasn't the First Baptist, Calvary Baptist, Sheppard's Baptist,

Holy Cross Baptist, Crown of Thorns Baptist or the Non-Catholic Baptist, but I can't remember if it was Second or Third) had a youth minister hauled off for child molesting. He blamed his misguided impulses on pornography. I was in my teens and had already seen enough nudie pictures and Sports Illustrated Swim Suit editions to know that, if anything, those magazines kept me on the straight and narrow. I'm not saying porn leaflets should be handed out with the offering envelope, but I was so intimidated and fascinated by the female body that I was too nervous to have a twosome until I was married!

The scariest church I've ever seen, and I'm including all cult-like churches, Southern Baptist Churches, and any scene with a church in any horror film, is the dilapidated God's Will Baptist Church north of Byron's Canoe Rental on Highway 23 North. This is the most frightening structure on the planet and must be the cosmic hole from which all shit-for-brain, Christ-crazy, inbred, turtle-fucking, radical Christian thought originates. Norman Bates probably had wet dreams about places like this. Jeffery Dahmer would have finally felt understood. The last time I drove by this particular house of the Lord, the church was in complete ruin, which I believed to be an aesthetic choice. The remaining paint was dried and cracked to the degree that the entire structure looked like it was covered with roaches doing complicated yoga posses. The shingles were tattered and ripped. The front porch was more like a trapdoor or secret entry to the hell within. The most memorable feature was the lawn décor. A series of tombstones sat in full view of every car that happened by. In all honesty, it looked like a Halloween haunted house, except scarier. But the kicker was the writing on the handcrafted plywood tombstones that were propped up loud and proud for every passing eyeball to take in. Brush-painted, blood-red inscriptions of Sinners go to hell, Satan is attacking, Adulterers are damned, Whores will burn, Abortion kills, Vengeance is the Lord's, and Church starts at 10 am, beckoned the weary and down-trodden to enter for a peaceful respite from the cruelties of a Godless society. Maybe I'm being too harsh, but I just didn't feel the love of Christ pouring out from this particular shit hole. Due to scheduling conflicts I, regrettably, have never been able to attend a Sunday service on North Hwy 23.

The church where I spent most of my time had only two little bitty moments that might garner a raised eyebrow. The day after the Pope was shot in 1981, I overheard a young Deacon say, "Someone almost did us a favor yesterday." It was the first time I realized that only Baptist have access to the road to heaven, and all other religious permeations were enemies who must be eradicated from our planet with vengeful love and humble destruction.

The other little hitch in our brotherhood came when a newly appointed youth minister, who had recently conquered his drug addiction, stole the money the youth choir had raised and ran away with the music minister's wife. Honestly, how could anyone have seen that coming? It was probably an honest mistake. Since the new guy was living with the music minister's family, his wife probably got confused, accidentally had sex with the wrong guy and unknowingly planned a gone-forever vacation. I wonder if she ever realized that the guy she left with wasn't her husband, or if she even remembered that she had three children. Oh, well, accidents happen, and it's always important to try to see things from the perspective of others.

Which reminds me…

Near my grandparents house was the Alamo Foundation. By near, I mean on the other side of the property line. The Alamos, headed up by Tony and Susan, were later charged with an entire slew of violations from tax evasion to child abuse. In the field behind my grandparents house was a series of dorm-like quarters where their faithful followers lived.

The Alamo Foundation later gained national attention when Susan passed to the other side (…of life that is, not the property line). Tony refused to turn her body over to the authorities saying that she would rise in three days. On day twelve, the neighbors started complaining about a stench in the air, and the show was over. Poor Tony ended up doing jail time on Federal charges. I always felt bad for Tony. I'm not good at magic tricks and slight-of-hand has never been my thing but you've got to admire his moxy to even attempt a Lazarus sequel.

There's one final church that I must mention. In a small town of 3,000 people, there were probably at least twenty churches from which a white person could choose to attend. There was one black church. Granted, the black population was tiny compared to the 2,971 whites that lived within city limits. Just across the street from the McNutt trailer park where I lived, was a small lot of land with two churches. One was all black, and the other was all white. I was approximately five or six years old at the time and never went to church. Sunday's were adventure days, and I was always out riding my bike or climbing down into the depths of the forbidden bluff behind our trailer.

One Sunday, while playing in some bushes behind the lot of the two churches, a black parishioner discovered me lurking around. He asked where my mama was and told me I needed to be in church. I had nothing else to do, so I thought I'd check out the show. The only thing I knew about these two churches was that the black church sang much louder than the white church. I remember thinking that I didn't look like any of the other people in the black church, but, since they didn't seem to care, I decided it was probably okay to be white. The music had a beat, and the people had rhythm. It was like Dance Fever without the guilt. The church was full of joy, and everyone seemed very happy to have me. For whatever reason, everyone asked how my mama was doing. I don't know why, but I'm reminded of the time that Opie did a guest spot on Good Times, or was that a dream?

A few weeks later, the white church extended an invitation to me. I can't honestly remember who invited me or when it happened. Perhaps I was lurking in their bushes or climbing in their tree. I guess it's possible that I was simply walking past the white church on my way to the black church. Anyway, somehow, I ended up in a church with people that looked more like me, but certainly seemed different. There was no dancing, no moving, no one even stood up to sing. From all I could tell, it must have been a good year for black folks because they were always celebrating. By contrast, the white church must have suffered through a long year of trial and tribulation, which was a popular topic in this particular sad-song parish.

A short time later, the black church burned down. I'm sure it was simply an electrical problem. It usually is. It was probably a neglected pot of coffee, an unattended cigarette, or, perhaps, a box of strike-anywhere matches stored too close to a box fan and a sheet of fifty-grade sandpaper sitting only a few inches from an open container of gasoline…these things can be much more dangerous than one would imagine. I later learned that the black congregation had found a new building on the outskirts of town. So, I guess everything worked out just fine.

I have no doubt that each church in my home town one has at least a few note-worthy moments in their illustrious history of serving the needs of their community. But of all the disturbing, disgusting things that have happened to me, or that I've even heard of for that matter, nothing has turned my stomach more than what I witnessed during my last visit home. For those with a weak stomach or those who become unsettled by graphic images, please stop reading now. I'm sure there's a folksy, friendlier, more charming story just a few pages away. But for those who like movies like Fight Club, Saw, or Sin City, let those disturbed minds read on.

Although I have no doubt this tale involves dirty money, back-scratching favors, extortion, and possibly sexual payoffs, I can't prove any of the aforementioned. All I know is that a preacher, a pious man of God, humble servant of the Lord, got himself a hummer in full view of the public. His congregation saw it, the community saw it, and the children saw it. I saw it. It wasn't your average back-alley, scab-kneed, hurry-before-someone-sees-me hummer. No, sir! This hummer was a humdinger. This hummer was a Hummer. I'm talking about a brand new candy-apple red, chrome-wheeled Hummer the size of a Special-Ed bus. And it was disgusting. A $60,000 vehicle parked in front of

$40,000 church paid for by a congregation of not more than sixty people who average, at most, $30,000 a year.

In a dying community where most people work the land with out-dated farm equipment and are forced to use a modified 1968 Volkswagen van to haul hay, a preacher drives an oversized, pimped-out war vehicle to get groceries and check his mail. Now, I may be wrong, but this dude must be getting some major tail. You've got to be some kind of player, owner of gold-plated brass balls to ask an impoverished congregation for the dough to spend on a whip like that. But here's the interesting part...the congregation agreed. I'm trying to imagine the moment when this spiritual leader pitched the idea. He must have worked some prominent church members for weeks in order to plant the idea and make his sheep think he needed such a monstrous ride. "I just hope people don't see me driving around town and feel sorry for me. Don't get me wrong, I love my F-150 but sometimes, when it rains, people give me sad looks 'cause they know I can't haul anything until the sun comes out. Now, I love my AM radio but a kick-ass Alpine would really let the people know that I love the Lord. Imagine the glory we'd send to God if our church were represented by a chrome-plated luggage rack and those neat little wheels that keep on spinning after you stop. Praise be! I'm not talking about something gaudy, after all, I'm a man of God and God's servants should be humble before all men, but that don't mean we cain't be classy. It's not like I'd represent us in a BMW or those high-maintenance Jags. No, sir. Simple sends a stronger message. Something that the people of Ozark can relate to. Something that says 'we are a church of hard workers, soldiers committed to defending and carrying on the word of the Lord'."

An astute parishioner may have replied, "How about a real nice Suburban? You know, one from Texas?" Pastor counters with, "Cleatus, the Lord is calling on me to make a much bolder move in this world of sinful materialism and shameful greed. Do you hear him? Listen to the Lord, Cleatus. He wants a Hummer. Cleatus, the Lord wants a Hummer."

And so it came to be that Cleatus went forth with the message from Pastor Assbag, singing and praising the glory which would befall all those who obeyed the calling of the Lord and did offer up with great abandon and zealous contribution to the rolling temple of humility decked with quadruple billion lumen spotlights which shall shower upon all the light of the Lord.

Renowned playwright Author Miller once wrote, "Cleave to no faith when faith brings blood." It's a great quote, but has significant timing problems. If faith brings blood then you've probably missed a crap load of red flags just before the slaughter. Perhaps a more helpful, although not quite as catchy, phrase would be, "Cleave to no faith when faith, or any person representing that faith, asks for money, touches your privates, asks you to keep secrets, makes you feel guilty for having completely natural thoughts, tells you they know God's intentions, tells you they can interpret the Bible, or any religious book, manuscript, poem, haiku, hieroglyphic, tea reading, palm reading, body language or dream; asks you to attack or hate another religion, tells you which God is right, claims to know the road to heaven, asks you to pick up the soap, has two-way conversations with the Lord, says sex is wrong, says thinking of sex is wrong, says divorce is wrong, believes that a woman should stay with a violent husband because it's God's will, ever interprets anything from the Bible to apply to issues not in the Bible like abortion, oil, guns, the environment, racism, whiskey; or has any opinion at all, no matter how insignificant, or relative, it may, or may never ever be regarding anything outside the scope of coming to the aide of people needing compassion, food or shelter."
Amen.

BED AND BREAKFAST

In 1992, while visiting Salem, Massachusetts, I toured the home were Nathaniel Hawthorne, author of The Scarlet Letter, was born. This historic location is now a museum with a gift shop and lots of neat plaques with interesting tidbits of information about the famous writer. In case my life-long luck changes and this book sells a ridiculous amount of copies, I feel that I should help those who may one day hope to cash in on the "Jerry slept here" industry, and find exactly which properties they should invest in.

My first home is still standing on highway 23 about four miles North of Ozark, Arkansas. It's the house on the left between the Pig Trough liquor store and *Dead Man's Curve*. Drunk drivers often miscalculate the rise and angle of this particular turn. It seems ironic that a liquor store and a landmark like *Dead Man's Curve* should happen to be in such close proximity. The house is an eight hundred square foot, two-story, settler-type home featuring a fireplace and a water-well just outside the back door. Interested buyers should note that this property is currently classified as a fixer-upper. Cattle often roam inside to escape the rain and springtime brings a variety of critters including opossums, raccoons, mice, and the occasional cottonmouth viper. The last time I drove by this home it was completely covered in kudzu, and the front door had fallen off the rusted hinges. However, there are still two windows with glass, and most of the stairs can support nearly sixty pounds of weight. Lots of potential here.

After a few months, the family moved into town to make it easier for Dad to pretend he was looking for job. Here's an interesting footnote – my first full sentence was spoken here. As the story goes, Mom and Dad were fighting and Dad had just thrown Mom across the room. She crashed into a closet door and fell to the ground. Apparently, my young mind interpreted all this rapid movement as a game and, wanting to participate, I flung my little body against the same closet door and dropped to the floor. As I looked at Mom, I became confused by her tears and made a simple suggestion, "Play mommy, don't cry." Many years later I drove by location-to-live number two, located on Third street about one half mile North of where the Magic Burger used to be, and thought, "That's a decent place."

Location-to-live number three was the beginning of progressive thinking. For starters, my mom divorced my dad. It's hard to say why. These things just happen and sometimes people grow apart. I'm not sure if it was the other women he was fucking, the drugs, the drinking, or the trip he took to Canada for two weeks and forgot to tell anyone he was leaving. Or, perhaps, it was the beatings. Like I said, people change as they mature and, by this time, mom was 21 and dad was 23. Regardless, Location-to-live number three was different because this place had no dad, but it did have wheels. Since we were destined to move a lot, a home with wheels made sense. We first parked our new home next to my grandparents place in Mulberry. A few months later, we rolled East down highway 64 to Clarksville, location-to-live # 4. Honestly, it would be difficult to justify a Bed and Breakfast in either of these two places since we drove off with the home. Perhaps a historical plaque with a donation jar would be more appropriate.

Location-to-live number 5 was significant. We were back in Ozark and had just rented a tiny rectangular lot in the McNutt trailer park. (Yes, this McNutt was a relation and, by all measures he was the best of the McNutt clan and a fascinating story in his own right. I should note that there was another McNutt trailer park on the East side of town but these people were of no relation. In a town of less then three thousand people there were two unrelated McNutt families in the trailer park business.) For a four year old, the trailer park was a magical place. I made many new friends here. Our favorite game was taking turns going down an enormous slide in the middle of the park. As you slid down the slide, a friend would toss you a rope that was tied to the top of the slide. If you could catch the rope, and climb back to the top of the slide, you got a bonus turn. Pure joy! (Note: That time that Sue Joe Ann took her turn going down the colossal slide and was supposed to catch the rope…but missed. Well, that was an accident. I can't be blamed for her not paying attention and just because the rope wrapped around her neck and left an awful multi-hued bruise does not mean I did it on purpose…no matter what her mom or the police officer said. Accidents happen. Learn to catch.) About eight feet from the back of our trailer home was a thirty-foot bluff with a creek that I was forbidden from ever going near or I would be beaten with the electric cord of mom's iron. I enjoyed countless hours of fun and adventure climbing up and down the bluff to play in the creek. More on this place later, and feel free to build a bed and breakfast here as this is where I was given and lost my favorite dog, momentarily defeated a giant of a bully, said "No," to the man who wanted me to rub lotion on his back, and saw my first naked female. The lovely lady was actually discovered in the pages of Playboy magazine. She was glorious cowgirl wearing a red cowboy hat, red cowboy boots and holding a lasso while sitting on a bale of hay. As mesmerized as I was by the magnificence of her strangely enticing body parts, I couldn't help thinking how uncomfortable it must be to sit naked on an itchy bale of hay.

Location-to-live number 6 marked a significant turn for me and Mother. Deciding that I needed a father figure, Mom married a man who met most of the qualifications a good dad should have. Well, he was male and that must have counted for something. He also had a bigger trailer. We had to move from the McNutt Trailer Park because it couldn't handle a ninety-footer. In case you're wondering, Ozark had no less than four trailer parks. Another deciding factor for my mom's union was that this man's son was one of my best friends. Of course, we hated each other immediately after the wedding.

Location-to-live #6 quickly gave way to #7 as we hitched-up our home to a semi, pulled it across the Arkansas River and moved out to the country. #7 was fantastic. It was just like those classic Boy and His Dog movies. My stepbrother and I spent every day hiking and discovering things like caves, dead animals, and discarded porn magazines. He quickly got bored with the woods and moved to California to live with his mother. The mountain then belonged to me and my imagination. (Truth be told, we rented, but my imagination pretended it was ours and we defended it with great courage.) Oh, the dogs? We had two, but both were hit by cars right away. About three hundred yards down the road was a Baptist church. I met a nice man there who introduced me to his friend, Jesus. It was at this tiny little church that I began learning all kinds of new and exciting things. For example, this is where I learned that black people came about because Cain murdered Abel and his punishment was to be turned black. Henceforth, all of his offspring were black. Ergo, all blacks are descendants of a murderer. Isn't it great what you can learn at church? By all means, build a really nice Bed and Breakfast here.

Location-to-live #8 put us back in city limits. This was a time consuming move because we sold the trailer and had to take things out of the mobile home and carry them to the new place, a home without wheels. However, the house we were supposed to move into was still occupied so we had a brief stay one block away. Location-to-live # 8 was short-lived but # 9 marked the first time a home felt permanent. By now I was fifteen and back in town. I started meeting people, real people with mouths and ears that I could talk to as opposed to the patient and friendly trees that had been my previous best friends and closest companions. This was the last place I would live until I graduated from high school. So, I suppose if any location-to-live is worthy of a Bed and Breakfast in my honor, it would be here. Although, to be honest, I don't think I ever actually wrote anything in any of the aforementioned places.

THE END.

ABOUT THE AUTHOR

Jerry McNutt is a graduate of the University of Central Arkansas, the University of Arkansas, and the University of Oklahoma. During those years of college, he acquired a B.S, M.A., and M.F.A. in theatre and directing. Since 1998, after moving to Los Angeles, Jerry has directed all sorts of reality television, short films, and a few commercials. When not directing, Jerry writes screenplays and books. But no matter how engrossed he becomes with writing, the typing stops when his two daughters need some daddy time.

www.ingramcontent.com/pod-product-compliance
Lightning Source LLC
Chambersburg PA
CBHW060511030426
42337CB00015B/1841